D0903627

A BOOK OF SERVICES

*The United Reformed Church
in England and Wales*

THE SAINT ANDREW PRESS
EDINBURGH
1980

First published 1980 by The Saint Andrew Press, 121 George Street, Edinburgh, on behalf of The Doctrine and Worship Committee of the United Reformed Church in England and Wales.

ISBN 07152 0446 7

Printed in Great Britain by Bell and Bain Ltd., Glasgow

Contents

5

Note: Responses by the people or individuals are indented and printed in bold type.

Preface

This book of services has been prepared at the request of the General Assembly of the United Reformed Church by its Doctrine and Worship Committee, for the use of ministers, lay preachers and others responsible for leading public worship.

Both the traditions which came together to form the United Reformed Church cherished freedom in worship. The publication of this book does not impugn that freedom. The orders found here are not prescribed. It is not expected that they will be used in our churches to the exclusion of others. Yet we believe most of these services reflect the ethos of our Church and of its inherited traditions. Some, for example ordination and induction, will be normative for such occasions in that those orders contain the accepted faith and practice of our Church.

The services have been widely used and welcomed in a draft form, and have now been revised in the light of comments received. One of our priorities has been to publish this book without too much delay. We hope that there may be something here to interest those of other traditions, but we offer this book primarily for use in our own Church, as a guide and enrichment to its worship and to the greater glory of God.

In the name of the Committee,

JOHN HUXTABLE
Chairman

May 1979.

Order of Worship

THE WORD AND THE PRAYERS

1 Scripture Sentences

2 Prayer of Approach

3 Hymn or Psalm

4 Confession of Sin

5 Assurance of Pardon

6 Gloria or Kyries

7 Prayer for Grace

8 Theme Introduction

9 Old Testament (and/or New Testament) Reading(s)

10 Psalm, Canticle, Hymn or Anthem

11 New Testament Reading (or Epistle and Gospel)

12 Sermon

13 Creed and/or Hymn

14 Notices

15 Special Acts (e.g. Baptism, Confirmation, Ordination, &c)

16 Prayers for the Church and the World

THE THANKSGIVING AND THE COMMUNION

A*

NOTES ON THE ORDER OF WORSHIP

Pattern

This order of worship consists of two parts: 'The Word and the Prayers' and 'The Thanksgiving and the Communion.' Because the normative order for worship in the Reformed tradition is a service of word and sacrament, what follows is offered as a pattern for the main Sunday worship of our churches. The outline can readily be modified on those occasions when communion is not celebrated. In any case ministers should feel free to vary the order and to substitute other prayers for those provided here, using if they wish extempore prayer; but it is hoped that, especially in the second part, this order will be followed.

Posture

How we do things as well as what we say is part of our worship, and indeed says something about what we believe. Suggestions are made in the order about the posture (standing, sitting, etc.) that might be adopted at different points. Some heighten the sense of a congregation acting together. All relate to the human posture naturally appropriate to what is happening. The 'body language' of the church is part of the fulness of offering ourselves to God. Leaders of worship should be careful to ensure that their bearing in the conduct of a service is helpful to the congregation.

The Entry

In many churches the Bible is carried into the church at the beginning of worship to remind the people that we can only meet God because he has first come to us. The record of his coming is in the Bible. It is appropriate for someone who is going to read from it to carry it in; or someone else may be appointed to do so. The preacher, as servant of the Word, should follow. The congregation might be encouraged to stand when the Bible is brought in, to give it due honour. The copy carried in should normally be the one to be read in worship. If it is placed open on the Table, a common custom, it may be taken to the place from which it is to be read immediately before the readings.

Prayer of Approach (2)

Whether this should come before or after the first hymn or psalm should be determined by the content of the prayer used and the hymn or psalm that is sung. A prayer of invocation, asking for God's blessing on the service, will usually come most appropriately before the first act of praise. A prayer of adoration or a prayer of thanksgiving, general or seasonal in character, may follow the first hymn or psalm, and in turn be followed by the prayer of confession.

Confession of Sin and Assurance of Pardon (4 and 5)

If a printed or duplicated service paper is provided for members of the congregation the prayer of confession can be said by the minister and people together. It is as important that God's pardon should be proclaimed as that we should confess our sins; and, though this will be done in the readings, sermon and communion, an assurance of pardon is appropriate after the confession.

Readings (9 and 11)

The order provides for readings from both Old and New Testaments. The best balance of scripture is normally obtained if there are three readings, one from the Old Testament and two from the New: Epistle and Gospel, though the traditional distinction between 'Epistle' and 'Gospel' is not easily sustained in the light of modern knowledge of the Bible. On occasion it may be convenient to omit the Old Testament reading and for both readings to be taken from the New Testament.

We recommend the use of the lectionary on page 172. This provides a 'controlling' lection for each Sunday or other day; and this should always be read, with one or both of the other readings provided.

Psalm, Canticle, Hymn or Anthem (10)

These should be so chosen as to be appropriate not only to the season or other occasion but also to their position in the service. The number of hymns suggested in the order may be varied.

If an anthem is sung it should be included at whatever point in the service it is most meaningful. If it is a scripture passage set to music it may on occasion serve as a substitute for one of the readings.

A selection of appropriate psalms can be found on page 182.

Sermon (12)

The message heard in the readings is made contemporary in the sermon. The traditional type of sermon may give place to some other form of proclamation, e.g. dialogue, drama or film.

The sermon may be followed by a period of silence and a short prayer, which may be a collect for the day if that has not been used already, or an ascription of praise. In general a greater use of silence in worship is to be encouraged.

Prayers (16)

Prayers for the Church and the world, which may vary in form, as indicated in the rubrics in the order, are placed, according to ancient tradition, after the readings and sermon. When we have heard God's word we respond to him in prayer for ourselves and for others. It has, however, long been customary in the churches which have come together in The United Reformed Church for general prayers of thanksgiving and intercession to be said after the readings and before the sermon. If so preferred, this order can be modified accordingly.

The Invitation and The Gracious Words (17)

In giving an invitation to the Lord's Supper the minister may make it clear that non-communicants are welcome and encouraged to stay through the service, but that if they prefer to do so they may leave during the next hymn, or at some other point which should be clearly specified. It is undesirable that there should be any break between the two parts of the service while a general exodus of non-communicants takes place; but people should not be left uncertain when they may leave if they so wish.

The Peace (18)

In addition to saying the words of The Peace the minister may give a handclasp to one or more persons near him, and this action may then be passed through the congregation, each member saying to his neighbour such words as 'Peace be with you.' Alternatively, each member of the congregation may turn to his neighbours and clasp hands and say, 'Peace be with you'.

The Narrative (21)

There should be unfailing use of the narrative of the institution when the Lord's Supper is celebrated. It may be read as a warrant before the eucharistic prayer, and/or used at the breaking of the bread; or it may be included within the eucharistic prayer (see below).

The Taking of the Bread and Wine (22)

At this point the minister may take the bread and the cup into his hands before giving thanks, or he may simply touch the bread and the cup to indicate that we are following the example of Christ with *this* bread and *this* cup.

The Thanksgiving/Eucharistic Prayer (23)

The basic elements and order of the eucharistic prayer are:

> the recital of the mighty acts of God in creation and redemption, often with special thanksgiving according to the season of the year;

> the commemoration with bread and wine of the sacrificial death and the resurrection of Christ 'until he come';

> invocation of the Holy Spirit, praying that what we do in obedience to Christ may be united to his perfect sacrifice and that we may be made one in him and receive the benefits of his passion and victory.

If the narrative of the institution is included in the eucharistic prayer (see above) it should come before the second section of the prayers, which logically follows from it.

If the actual wording of the prayers given in this order is not used, care should be taken to ensure that the full content of the eucharistic prayer is included in the service.

Congregations not accustomed to saying the responsive parts of the prayer can quickly learn them; but where they are not used the minister may introduce the prayer by saying 'Let us lift up our hearts and give thanks to the Lord our God'.

The Lord's Prayer (24)

The version of the Lord's Prayer given here is that to be found in the Church of England's new *Alternative Service Book* and is used with permission. This differs in the final petition 'lead us not into temptation' from that in *New Church Praise* (1st edn.). It is suggested that copies of the hymnbook may be amended.

The Sharing of the Bread and Wine (26)

Ministers, elders and people share the bread and wine; and it does not matter in what order this is done. The minister may receive first, then the elders and then the people, so that the communion spreads from the Table; or the bread and wine may be taken to the people, so that they are served first, and then the elders, and the minister last. All may eat the bread and drink the wine as they are served; or all may eat, or drink, at the same time.

What is more important than the order in which minister, elders and people receive communion is that, as far as possible, the bread and wine should be passed through the congregation, so that each person serves his neighbour and the corporate character of the communion is thus expressed. The sharing is done most simply and meaningfully when a single piece of bread and a common cup are passed.

Going Out

It makes for a seemly end to worship if the Bible, the gifts of money and the communion vessels are carried out of the church, the minister and people following. In this way we proclaim that our service continues in everyday life in God's world.

Order of Worship

THE WORD AND THE PRAYERS

The Bible may be brought into the church, all standing; and the minister enters and may call the people to worship saying,

Let us worship God.

1 Scripture Sentences *(all standing)*

This is the day which the Lord has made;
let us rejoice and be glad in it.
It is good to give thanks to the Lord;
for his love endures for ever.

Other sentences may be used or seasonal sentences added. The readings or psalms for the day may suggest such sentences, of which the following are examples:

General

Our help is in the name of the Lord, who made heaven and earth.

God is spirit, and those who worship him must worship in spirit and in truth.

In everything by prayer and supplication with thanksgiving let your requests be made known to God.

Be always joyful; pray continually; give thanks whatever happens; for this is what God in Christ wills for you.

Advent

The glory of the Lord shall be revealed, and all mankind together shall see it; for the Lord himself has spoken.

Shout aloud and rejoice; I am coming, and I will make my dwelling among you, says the Lord.

Christmas

Unto us a child is born, unto us a son is given.

God is love: and his love was disclosed to us in this, that he sent his only Son into the world to bring us life.

Epiphany

The grace of God has dawned upon the world with healing for all mankind.

God was in Christ reconciling the world to himself, and has entrusted us with the message of reconciliation.

Lent

Compassion and forgiveness belong to the Lord our God, though we have rebelled against him.

Jesus said: If any man would come after me, let him deny himself and take up his cross and follow me.

Passiontide

Christ humbled himself, and in obedience accepted even death—death on a cross.

Christ himself bore our sins in his body on the tree, that we might die to sin and live to righteousness. By his wounds you have been healed.

Easter

Christ being raised from the dead will never die again; death no longer has dominion over him.

Praise be to the God and Father of our Lord Jesus Christ, who in his great mercy gave us new birth into a living hope by the resurrection of Jesus Christ from the dead!

God be praised, he gives us the victory through our Lord Jesus Christ.

Ascension

The Lord reigns! Let the heavens be glad, and let the earth rejoice.

Christ has entered into heaven itself, now to appear in the presence of God on our behalf.

Pentecost

God's love has been poured into our hearts through the Holy Spirit he has given us.

Here is the proof that we dwell in God and God dwells in us: he has imparted his Spirit to us.

Trinity

Holy, holy, holy is God, the sovereign Lord of all, who was, and is, and is to come.

All Saints

Since we are surrounded by so great a cloud of witnesses, let us lay aside every weight, and the sin which clings so closely, and let us run with perseverance the race that is set before us, looking to Jesus the pioneer and perfecter of our faith.

Harvest

The earth is the Lord's and all that is in it, the world and those who dwell therein.

While earth lasts seedtime and harvest, cold and heat, summer and winter, day and night, shall never cease.

Old and New Year

Be strong and of good courage; be not frightened, neither be dismayed; for the Lord your God is with you wherever you go.

The Lord will guard your going and your coming, now and for evermore.

2 Prayer of Approach

This prayer may be said before or after the first hymn or psalm

Let us pray

Almighty God,
to whom all hearts are open,
all desires known,
and from whom no secrets are hid:
cleanse the thoughts of our hearts
by the inspiration of your Holy Spirit,
that we may perfectly love you,
and worthily magnify your holy Name;
through Christ our Lord. **Amen.**

Or this prayer may be used:

Almighty God, infinite and eternal
in wisdom, power and love:
we praise you for all that you are,
and for all that you do for the world.
You have shown us your truth and your love
in our Saviour Jesus Christ.

Help us by your Spirit
to worship you in spirit and in truth;
through Jesus Christ our Lord. **Amen.**

3 Hymn or Psalm

4 Confession of Sin

Let us confess our sins to God and ask his
forgiveness.

**Lord God most merciful,
we confess that we have sinned,
through our own fault,
and in common with others,
in thought, word and deed,
and through what we have left undone.**

We ask to be forgiven.

**By the power of your Spirit
turn us from evil to good,
help us to forgive others,
and keep us in your ways
of righteousness and love;
through Jesus Christ our Lord. Amen.**

5 Assurance of Pardon

In repentance and in faith
receive the promise of grace
and the assurance of pardon:

Here are words you may trust,
words that merit full acceptance:
'Christ Jesus came into the world to save sinners.'
Your sins are forgiven for his sake.

Thanks be to God.

Or this Assurance may be used:

> God so loved the world
> that he gave his only Son,
> that whoever believes in him
> should not perish
> but have eternal life.
>
> To all who repent and believe,
> we declare, in the name of the Father,
> the Son and the Holy Spirit:
> God grants you
> the forgiveness of your sins.
>
> **Thanks be to God.**

6 Gloria in excelsis *(all standing)*

> **Glory to God in the highest,**
> **and peace to his people on earth.**
>
> **Lord God, heavenly King,**
> **almighty God and Father,**
> **we worship you, we give you thanks,**
> **we praise you for your glory.**
>
> **Lord Jesus Christ, only Son of the Father,**
> **Lord God, Lamb of God,**
> **you take away the sin of the world:**
> **have mercy on us;**
> **you are seated at the right hand of the Father:**
> **receive our prayer.**
>
> **For you alone are the Holy One,**
> **you alone are the Lord,**
> **you alone are the Most High,**
> **Jesus Christ, with the Holy Spirit,**
> **in the glory of God the Father. Amen.**

The Kyries (*may be said in place of the Gloria in excelsis*)

Lord, have mercy on us.

Christ, have mercy on us.
Lord, have mercy on us.

7 Prayer for Grace

The collect of the day or other prayer for grace may be said here or after the sermon.

8 Theme Introduction

The Minister may then introduce the theme of the day's service, and may speak in particular to the children, and a hymn may be sung before the church departments separate; or the minister may speak to the children after one of the readings.

9 Old Testament Reading

and/or a New Testament Reading

10 Psalm, Canticle, Hymn or Anthem

11 New Testament Reading

or readings: Epistle and Gospel

A hymn may be sung.

12 Sermon

The sermon may be followed by a silence and/or a prayer. If a creed is used it should be said at this point, or the hymn following might affirm the faith of the Church.

13 Hymn

14 The notices *may be given here or after the prayers.*

15 Special Acts, *such as Baptism, Confirmation, Ordination may take place at this point.*

16 Prayers for the Church and the World

After each paragraph a versicle and response may be said, such as

> Lord, in your mercy,
> **Hear our prayer.**

The special subjects after the words 'We pray for' are merely suggestions; others may be substituted; omissions may be made. Intervals of silence should be kept.

The paragraphs may be used as a continuous prayer by the omission of the words 'We pray for' and the words in italics.

> Let us pray.

> Almighty God,
> whose Spirit helps us in our weakness
> and guides us in our prayers;
> we pray for the Church and for the world
> in the name of Jesus Christ.

> We pray for

the Church throughout the world
our ministers, elders and members
local unity and witness

> Renew the faith and life of the Church;
> strengthen its witness;
> and make it one in Christ.

Grant that we
and all who confess that he is Lord
may be faithful in service
and filled with his spirit,
and that the world may be turned to him.

We pray for

the nations of the world
our own country
all who work for reconciliation

Guide the nations
in the ways of justice, liberty and peace;
and help them to seek
the unity and welfare of mankind.
Give to our Queen and to all in authority
wisdom to know and strength to do
what is right.

We pray for

those in trade and industry
members of the professions
all who serve the community

Grant that men and women in their various callings
may have grace to do their work well;
and may the resources of the earth be wisely used,
truth honoured and preserved,
and the quality of our life enriched.

We pray for

the sick and the suffering
victims of injustice
the lonely and the bereaved

Comfort those in sorrow;
heal the sick in body or in mind;
and deliver the oppressed.

Give us active sympathy
for all who suffer; and help us
so to bear the burdens of others
that we may fulfil the law of Christ.

We pray for

our families
friends and neighbours
all who need our prayers

Keep us and the members of our families
united in loyalty and in love,
and always in your care;
and may our friends and neighbours,
and all for whom we pray,
receive the help they need,
and live in peace.

We remember those who have died.

Eternal God, accept our thanks and praise
for all who have served you faithfully here on earth,
and especially for those dear to our own hearts . . .

May we and all your people,
past, present and to come,
share the life and joy of your kingdom;
through Jesus Christ our Lord. **Amen.**

The notices, if not already given, may be given here.

THE THANKSGIVING AND THE COMMUNION

17 The Invitation and the Gracious Words

*The minister may then give an invitation to those present,
to whatever branch of the Church they belong, to share in
the Lord's Supper.*

Hear the gracious words of
our Lord Jesus Christ:

Come to me,
all who labour and are heavy-laden,
and I will give you rest.

I am the bread of life;
he who comes to me shall not hunger,
and he who believes in me shall never thirst.

Him who comes to me
I will not cast out.

18 The Peace

The peace of the Lord Jesus Christ
be with you all.
    Peace be with you.

19 Offertory

The offerings of the people are collected.

All stand when the offering are brought to the Table.

The bread and wine may be carried into the church and brought to the Table; or, if they have been prepared on the Table before the service begins, the bread and wine are uncovered.

Then a prayer is said, all standing.

Let us pray.

Eternal God,
we come with these gifts
to offer our sacrifice of praise
and the service of our lives;
    through Jesus Christ our Lord. Amen.

20 Hymn

This hymn may be sung while the money, bread and wine are brought to the Table, in which case the offertory prayer follows the hymn.

21 The Narrative of the Institution

The narrative need not be read here if it is used at the breaking of the bread or if it is incorporated in the Thanksgiving.

Hear the narrative of the institution
of the Lord's Supper as it was recorded
by the apostle Paul.

I received from the Lord what I also delivered
to you, that the Lord Jesus
on the night when he was betrayed
took bread, and when he had given thanks,
he broke it, and said,
'This is my body which is for you.
Do this in remembrance of me.'
In the same way also
the cup, after supper, saying,
'This cup is the new covenant in my blood.
Do this, as often as you drink it,
in remembrance of me.'
For as often as you eat this bread
and drink the cup, you proclaim the Lord's death
until he comes.

22 The Taking of the Bread and Wine

In the name of the Lord Jesus Christ,
and following his example,
we take this bread and this cup,
and give thanks to God.

23 The Thanksgiving I (*all standing*)

Lift up your hearts.
We lift them to the Lord.
Let us give thanks to the Lord our God.
It is right to give him thanks and praise.

With joy we give you thanks and praise,
Almighty God, Source of all life and love,
that we live in your world,
that you are always
creating and sustaining it by your power,
and that you have so made us
that we can know and love you,
trust and serve you.

We give you thanks
that you loved the world so much
that you gave your only Son,
so that everyone who has faith in him
may not die but have eternal life.

*Here may follow a seasonal or other special thanksgiving
of which the following are examples:*

General

We thank you that Jesus was born among us;
that he lived our common life on earth;
that he suffered and died for us;
that he rose again;
and that he is always present
through the Holy Spirit.

We thank you that we can live in the faith
that your kingdom will come,
and that in life, in death
and beyond death you are with us.

Advent

We praise you
that through his coming
your promises given by the prophets were fulfilled,
and that the day of our deliverance has dawned;
and, as we look for the triumph of his kingdom,
we exult with holy joy.

Christmas

We praise you
that he took our nature
and was born as the child of Mary,
that he might share our life,
reveal your love, and reconcile us to yourself,
and give us power to become your children.

Epiphany

We praise you
that he is the Light of the world
through whom we are brought
out of darkness into light,
and that by him your glory has been revealed
to the nations.

Lent

We praise you
that because of his likeness to us
he was tested every way yet without sin,
and that having endured and overcome temptation
he is able to help us in our times of trial,
and to give us strength to take up the cross
and follow him.

Passiontide

We praise you
that for us and for our salvation
he humbled himself
and in obedience accepted even death—death on a cross;
and that he bore our sins in his body on the tree
that we being dead to sin should live to righteousness.

Easter

We praise you
that after he had suffered
and been put to death on the Cross
he was raised from the dead by your power;
that he is the true Passover Lamb
who takes away the sin of the world;
and that by his glorious resurrection
he has restored to us eternal life
and given us the joy of your kingdom.

Ascension

We praise you
that having suffered and died for us
and being raised from the dead
he lives and reigns for ever in your glory,
and so fulfils his promise to be with us always,
to the end of time.

Pentecost

We praise you
that according to the promise of Christ
the Holy Spirit came to fill the Church with power;
and that he comes to us today
that we being renewed and united by him
may be strong to proclaim the Gospel in the world.

Then the prayer continues

Therefore with all the company of heaven,
and with all your people,
of all places and times,
we proclaim your greatness and sing your praise.

Holy, holy, holy Lord
God of power and might,
Heaven and earth are full of your glory.
Hosanna in the highest.

Blessed is he
who comes in the name of the Lord.
Hosanna in the highest.

Holy Lord God,
by what we do here
in remembrance of Christ
we celebrate
    his perfect sacrifice on the Cross
    and his glorious resurrection and ascension;
we declare
    that he is Lord of all;
and we prepare for
    his coming in his kingdom.

We pray that
through your Holy Spirit
this bread may be for us
    the body of Christ
and this wine
    the blood of Christ.

Accept our sacrifice of praise;
and as we eat and drink
at his command
unite us to Christ
as one body in him,
and give us strength
to serve you in the world.

And to you,
one holy and eternal God,
Father, Son and Holy Spirit,
we give praise and glory,
now and for ever.   **Amen.**

The prayer concludes with the Lord's Prayer as on page
37.

The Thanksgiving II (*all standing*)

Lift up your hearts
   We lift them up to the Lord
Let us give thanks to the Lord our God
   It is right to give him thanks and praise

Almighty God, Eternal Father,
it is our duty and delight
at all times and in all places
to give you thanks and praise.
You are the creator of all things
and the source of all life,
in whom we live and move and have our being.
You have given us your only Son, Jesus Christ,
to free us from the slavery of sin
and to make us heirs of eternal life.
He was born as one of us,
was obedient to your will,
and accepted death upon the cross:
you raised him from the dead
and have made him Lord of all.
You send us your Spirit
   to guide us into the truth,
   to bring us reconciliation and peace,
   and to renew us as the Body of your Son.

(And now we give you thanks . . .)

We praise you for you are God.

**We acclaim you, for you are the Lord.
We worship you, eternal Father:
and with the whole company of heaven
we sing in endless praise:
Holy, holy, holy Lord,
God of power and might.
Heaven and earth are full of your glory.
Hosanna in the highest.**

**Blessed is he who comes in the name of the
Lord.
Hosanna in the highest.**

Heavenly Father,
we offer you this praise
through Jesus Christ, your only Son, our Lord,
who hallowed your name,
accomplished your will,
established your kingdom,
and gave himself to be our spiritual food.
And now we pray that by the power of your Holy
    Spirit
these gifts of bread and wine
may be to us his body and his blood.
For on the night when he was betrayed
he took bread, and when he had given thanks,
he broke it, and said,
'Take, eat: this is my body which is for you.
Do this in remembrance of me.'
In the same way after supper, he took the cup, saying,
'This cup is the new covenant in my blood.
Do this, as often as you drink it,
in remembrance of me.'
Therefore, heavenly Father,
obeying the command of your dear Son,
and looking for his coming again in glory,
we celebrate the perfect sacrifice of his death upon the
    cross,
his mighty resurrection and his glorious ascension.

Christ is Victor.
Christ is King.
Christ is Lord of all.

Father, accept through Christ
our sacrifice of thanks and praise:
and as we eat and drink these holy gifts,
kindle in us the fire of your Spirit
that with the whole Church on earth and in heaven
we may be made one in him.

B

Count us worthy
to stand before you as your people
and to offer without ceasing our adoration and service,
through Jesus Christ our Lord.
Through him, with him, and in him,
in the unity of the Holy Spirit,
all honour and glory are yours, Father Almighty,
now and for ever.   **Amen.**

*The prayer concludes with The Lord's Prayer as on
page* 37.

The Thanksgiving III *(all standing)*

Lift up your hearts
We lift them up to the Lord.
Let us give thanks to the Lord our God
It is right to give him thanks and praise.

We thank you,
Lord God almighty,
that you are a God of people,
that you are not ashamed
to be called our God,
that you know us all by name
that you hold the world in your hands.
You have created us
and called us in this life
that we should be made one with you
to be your people here on earth.
Blessed are you,
creator of all that is,
Blessed are you
for giving us space and time for living.
Blessed are you
for the light of our eyes
and for the air we breathe.
We thank you for the whole of creation,

for all the works of your hands,
for all that you have done among us
through Jesus Christ, our Lord.
Therefore, together with all the living
and all who have gone before us in faith,
we praise your name,
O Lord our God,
bowing before you
adoring you, saying:

**Holy, holy, holy Lord,
God of power and might,
heaven and earth are full of your glory.
Hosanna in the highest.
Blessed is he who comes in the name of the
Lord.
Hosanna in the highest.**

We thank you, holy father,
Lord our God,
for Jesus Christ,
your beloved son,
whom you called and sent
to serve us and give us light,
to bring your kingdom to the poor,
to bring redemption to captives
and to be for ever
and for us all
the likeness and embodiment
of your constant love and goodness.
We thank you
for this unforgettable man
who has fulfilled everything that is human—
our life, our death.
We thank you
because he gave himself,
heart and soul, to this world.

For, on the night that he was delivered up,
he took bread into his hands
and raising his eyes to you,
God, his almighty father,
he gave thanks
and broke the bread
and delivered it among his friends
with the words:
take and eat,
this is my body for you.
Do this in memory of me.

He also took the cup
and, giving thanks to you, said:
this cup is the new covenant in my blood
shed for you and for all
for the forgiveness of sins.
Every time you drink this cup,
you shall do it in memory of me.

So whenever we eat of this bread
and drink from this cup,
we proclaim the death of the Lord
until he comes.

Therefore, Lord our God,
we present this sign of our faith
and therefore we call to mind now
the suffering and death of your son,
his resurrection from the dead,
his entry into your glory,
rejoicing that he
who is exalted at your right hand
will speak up for us
and will come
to do justice to the living and the dead
on the day that you have appointed.

We beseech you
send among us your Holy Spirit

and give a new face
to this earth that is dear to us.
Let there be peace
wherever people live,
the peace that we cannot make ourselves
and that is more powerful than all violence,
your peace like a bond,
a new covenant between us all,
the power of Jesus Christ
here among us.

Then your name will be made holy,
Lord our God,
through him and with him and in him
everywhere on earth
and in this fellowship of the Holy Spirit
this hour and all the days
into eternity.   **Amen.**

24 The Lord's Prayer

And now, as Jesus taught us, we say

**Our Father in heaven
hallowed be your Name,
your kingdom come,
your will be done,
on earth as in heaven.
Give us today our daily bread.
Forgive us our sins
as we forgive those who sin against us.
Lead us not into temptation
but deliver us from evil.
For the Kingdom, the power, and the glory
   are yours
now and for ever.   Amen.**

25 The Breaking of the Bread (all sit)

The Lord Jesus
on the night when he was betrayed
took bread (hear the minister takes the
bread in his hands), and when he had given thanks,
he broke it (here the minister
breaks the bread), and said,
'This is my body which is for you.
Do this in remembrance of me.'

In the same way also the cup (here the minister
raises the cup), saying
'This cup is the new covenant in my blood.
Do this, as often as you drink it,
in remembrance of me.'

Or, if the narrative of the institution has been used earlier
in the service, as he breaks the bread the minister may say:

The bread which we break
is the communion of the body of Christ.

And as he pours the wine and raises the cup he may say:

The cup of blessing which we bless
is the communion of the blood of Christ.

26 The Sharing of the Bread and Wine

In giving the bread the minister says:

Take, eat; this is the body of Christ
which is broken for you;
do this in remembrance of him.

or,

The body of our Lord Jesus Christ,
given for you.

In giving the cup the minister says:

This cup is the new covenant
in the blood of Christ,
shed for you and for all
for the remission of sins:
drink of it.

or,

The blood of our Lord Jesus **Christ**,
shed for you.

27 **Acclamation** (*may be said or sung*)

Let us praise the Lord.

Christ has died.
Christ is risen.
In Christ shall all be made alive.

Blessing and honour and glory and
power be to our God for ever and
ever.   Amen.

28 **Prayer after Communion**

Let us pray.

Most gracious God,
we praise you
for what you have given
and for what you have promised us here.

You have made us one
with all your people
in heaven and on earth.
You have fed us
with the bread of life,
and renewed us for your service.

Now we give ourselves to you;
and we ask
that our daily living
may be part of the life of your kingdom,
and that our love
may be your love reaching out into the life of the
world;
through Jesus Christ our Lord.   **Amen.**

28 Hymn or Doxology

29 Dismissal and Blessing

Go in peace to serve the Lord;
and the blessing of God Almighty,
the Father, the Son and the Holy Spirit,
be with you always.   **Amen.**

One of the following seasonal blessings may be used

Advent

Go in peace to serve the Lord,
confident that all in heaven and on earth
is to be brought into a unity in Christ;
and the blessing....

Christmas

Go in peace to serve the Lord.
May Christ be born in your hearts
and dwell among you;
and the blessing....

Epiphany

Go in peace to serve the Lord
who is Saviour of all mankind;
and the blessing....

Lent

Go in peace to serve the Lord
in obedience and humility;
and the blessing . . . .

Passiontide

Go in peace to serve the Lord,
remembering that you are not your own
but were bought at a price;
and the blessing . . . .

Easter

Go in peace to serve the Lord,
knowing that because he lives
your labour cannot be lost;
and the blessing . . . .

or

Go in peace to serve the Lord;
May the God of peace,
who brought up from the dead our Lord Jesus,
the great Shepherd of the sheep,
by the blood of the eternal covenant,
make you perfect in all goodness
so that you may do his will,
and may he make of us what he would have us be
through Jesus Christ, to whom be glory
for ever and ever. **Amen.**

Ascension

Go in peace to serve the Lord
whose name is above every name;
and the blessing . . . .

B*

Pentecost

Go in peace to serve the Lord
in the power of the Holy Spirit;
and the blessing....

or

May God, the Giver of hope,
fill you with all joy and peace
because you trust in him.
so that you may have abundant hope
through the power of the Holy Spirit;
and the blessing....

Trinity

Go in peace to serve the Lord
on whom our faith depends from start to finish;
and the blessing....

or

The grace of our Lord Jesus Christ,
and the love of God,
and the fellowship of the Holy Spirit
be with you all. **Amen.**

All Saints

Go in peace to serve the Lord
who has promised that there will be
one flock and one shepherd
and that nothing can snatch us from his care;
and the blessing....

Harvest

Go in peace to serve the Lord.
As the Father sent the Son,
so the Son sends you;
and the blessing....

or

Go in peace to serve the Lord
as trustworthy stewards of all he has to give;
and the blessing....

Old and New Year

Go in peace to serve the Lord
who is the same yesterday,
today and for ever,
and whose unswerving love is renewed every morning;
and the blessing....

Baptism of Infants

Baptism should normally be administered in the presence of the congregation. It may precede or follow the prayers for the Church and the world, and so be brought into close relation to prayers, offertory (and communion).

1 Introduction

The minister says:

> We are met as a congregation of God's people to administer the Sacrament of Baptism to N... the son/daughter of A and C.

We read in the Bible that, at the beginning of his ministry, our Lord was baptized by John in the river Jordan, so identifying himself with our sinful humanity. His baptism found fulfilment in the Cross, where he gave himself for the life of the world.

After his resurrection, he commanded his disciples to preach the Gospel to all nations and to baptize; and we read that on the day of Pentecost Peter said to the people:

> Repent, and be baptized every one of you in the name of Jesus Christ for the forgiveness of your sins; and you shall receive the gift of the Holy Spirit. For the promise is to you and to your children and to all that are far off, every one whom the Lord our God calls to him. *Acts 2: 38-39*

This sacrament is a sign and seal of the covenant of grace, which God has made with us in Christ. By baptism we are received into his Church. Christ brings us from death to life so that, having been raised to life with him, we may live as heirs of his kingdom.

The children of Christian parents, through they may not understand these things, are within the covenant and belong to the life of the Church. Christ claims them as his own, calling them to him and saying:

Let the children come to me, do not hinder them; for to such belongs the kingdom of God.

Mark 10: 14 (RSV)

Since this *child* is not yet of an age to speak for *himself*, *his* parent(s) (and godparents) and the church must make promises, so that through Christian nurture *he* may come to make *his* own profession of faith and serve Christ in the Church and the world.

2 The Promises

Then the minister, addressing the parents of the child to be baptized, says:

So, in presenting this child for baptism
Do you confess your faith in one God,
Father, Son and Holy Spirit,
taking the Father to be your Father,
the Son to be your Saviour and Lord
the Spirit to be your Helper and Guide?

I do/We do

Do you promise, by God's help, to provide a
Christian home for this child and to bring *him* up in
the faith of the Gospel and the fellowship of the
Church?

I do/We do

If there are godparents or sponsors present the minister says to them:

> Do you, the godparents/sponsors of this child,
> confess your faith in God, Father, Son and Holy
> Spirit;
> and do you undertake to help the parents of this child
> in every way you can to bring *him* up in the faith
> of the Gospel and the fellowship of the Church?

I do/We do

The minister then addresses the following question to the congregation:

> Do you, as a congregation of God's people, promise to
> play your part in the Christian upbringing of *this child*
> by providing instruction in the Gospel of God's love,
> the example of Christian faith and character, and the
> strong support of the family of God in fellowship,
> prayer and service?

We do

3 Prayer *follows, the minister saying:*

Let us pray.

> Almighty and eternal God we give you thanks
> for our life and salvation in Jesus your Son,
> who became one of us
> and died and rose again
> that we might have life in him
> and be made members of your Church
> and heirs of your kingdom.
> Be with us in the power of your Spirit
> and so use this water
> and our obedience to Christ
> that *N* ... whom we baptize in your Name

may receive the fulness of your grace
and always remain in the number of your faithful
people;
through Jesus Christ our Lord.   **Amen.**

or,

Almighty and eternal God
in your infinite mercy and goodness
you have promised
that you will not only be our God
but also the God and Father of our children.
We pray that
as you have called us to share in your mercy
in the fellowship of faith
so you will receive *this child*
whom we bring to you now.
Be with us in the power of your Spirit
and so use this water
and our obedience to Christ
that *N* ... whom we baptize in your Name
may receive the fulness of your grace
and always remain in the number of your faithful
people;
through Jesus Christ our Lord.   **Amen.**

4 The Baptism

*Then, the congregation standing, the minister may receive
the child from* **his** *father and pours or sprinkles water on*
his *head, saying:*

N ... I baptize you in the Name of the Father and
of the Son and the Holy Spirit.   **Amen.**

Then the minister says, or the congregation may sing:

**The Lord bless you and keep you;
the Lord make his face to shine upon you
and be gracious unto you;
the Lord lift up his countenance upon you
and give you peace.   Amen.**

The minister then presents the newly-baptized child before the congregation, and says to the people:

You are witnesses that *N . . .* has been received into the family and household of God (or, into the membership of the Christian Church) and I call on you
to pray for *him* and to care for *him*, that *he* may grow in Christian faith and life, and continue in Christ's service all *his* days.

The minister then returns the child to his mother and may say:

The Lord be with you in the high and holy duty he has laid upon you, and abundantly fulfil in you his word: Whoever receives one such little child in my name receives me. *Mark 9:37 (RSV)*

5 Prayer *follows, in such words as these:*

Heavenly Father
we give you thanks
for receiving *this little child* by baptism
into the life of your Church.
Keep *him* always in your love;
grant that *he* may grow strong in body and in mind;
protect *him* in all dangers and temptations;
and bring *him* to faith in Jesus Christ as *his* Saviour
        and Lord.
We ask your blessing on the parents (and godparents) of this child.
Help them to surround *him* with the love and security
        he needs;
give them grace and wisdom to teach *him* your truth
        and to lead *him* in your way;
and through their love for *him* may they learn to love
        you more.

We commend to you their home and all the families
    of this congregation.
Grant that in our homes
we may honour you and love and serve each other.
Accept us as we recall our own baptism
and rededicate ourselves to you;
and help us to care for all who are one with us
in the life of your Church;
through Jesus Christ our Lord. **Amen.**

Baptism of Believers and Confirmation

In the case of someone making a profession of faith, Baptism and Confirmation should be seen as two parts of a whole act. This act should normally take place in the presence of the congregation. It may precede or follow the prayers for the Church and the world, and so be brought into close relation to prayers, offertory (and communion).

1 Introduction

The minister says

We are met as a congregation of God's people to administer the Sacrament of Baptism to AB (CD, EF...). [With NO(PQ, RS...) who *was* previously baptized into the family and household of God, and engaged to be the Lord's] *he* will be received into the full privileges and responsibilities of membership of the Church, and in particular into membership of this congregation.

We read in the Bible that, at the beginning of his ministry, our Lord was baptized by John in the river Jordan, so identifying himself with our sinful humanity. His baptism found fulfilment in the Cross, where he gave himself for the life of the world.

After his resurrection, he commanded his disciples to preach the Gospel to all nations and to baptize; and we read that on the day of Pentecost Peter said to the people:

> Repent, and be baptized every one of you in the
> name of Jesus Christ for the forgiveness of your
> sins; and you shall receive the gift of the Holy
> Spirit. For the promise is to you and to your
> children and to all that are far off, every one whom
> the Lord our God calls to him.   *Acts 2: 38–39*

This sacrament is a sign and seal of the covenant of
grace, which God has made with us in Christ. By
baptism we are received into his Church. Christ
brings us from death to life so that, having been
raised to life with him, we may live as heirs of his
kingdom.

2 The Promises

*The candidates come forward and as they stand facing him
the minister says to them*

A (C, E, . . .) (N, P, R . . .) you now come in
response to the call of Christ and the leading of the
Holy Spirit, to make your profession of the
Christian Faith, and to accept the responsibilities
and privileges of membership. Let us hear, then, in
the presence of God, that you turn to Christ, that
you confess your faith in God, and that you intend,
in dependence on the help of his Spirit to live as
faithful members of the Church and to serve him in
the world.

A . . . I ask you in the presence of God and before this
congregation:

Do you repent of your sins, renounce evil and turn to
Christ?

I do

Do you confess your faith in one God, Father, Son
and Holy Spirit,

taking the Father to be your Father,
the Son to be your Saviour and Lord,
the Spirit to be your Helper and Guide?

I do

Do you promise, in dependence on God's grace,
to be faithful in private and public worship;
to live in the fellowship of the Church and to share in
      its work;
and to give and serve, as God enables you, for the
advancement of his kingdom throughout the world?

I do

Do you promise, by that same grace, to follow Christ
and to seek to do and to bear his will all the days
of your life?

I do

And do you trust in his mercy alone to bring you into
the fulness of the life of the world to come?

I do

Or the following form may be used:

A ... I ask you in the presence of God and before this
      congregation:
Do you repent of your sins, renounce evil and turn to
      Christ?

I do

Then will you declare your faith and commitment?

The candidate says:

**I confess my faith
in one God, Father, Son and Holy Spirit,
taking the Father to be my Father,
the Son to be my Saviour and Lord,
the Spirit to be my Helper and Guide.**

I promise
in dependence on God's grace,
to be faithful in private and public worship;
to live in the fellowship of the Church
and to share in its work;
and to give and serve, as God enables me,
for the advancement of his kingdom
throughout the world.
I promise, by that same grace,
to follow Christ
and to seek to do and to bear his will
all the days of my life;
and I trust in his mercy alone
to bring me into the fulness
of the life of the world to come.

3 *The candidates for Baptism kneel or stand by the place of baptism.*
The congregation stands.

Prayer follows, the minister saying:

Let us pray.

Almighty and eternal God we give you thanks
for our life and salvation in Jesus your Son,
who became one of us
and died and rose again
that we might have life in him
and be made members of your Church
and heirs of your kingdom.
Be with us in the power of your Spirit
and so use this water
and our obedience to Christ
that *A* ... whom we baptize in your Name
may receive the fulness of your grace
and always remain in the number of your faithful
        people;
through Jesus Christ our Lord.   **Amen.**

4 The Baptism

*The congregation standing, the candidate kneels or stands
and the minister pours or sprinkles water on his/her head,
saying:*

> *A ...* I baptize you in the Name of the Father, and of
> the Son, and of the Holy Spirit. **Amen.**

Then the minister says, or the congregation may sing:

> **The Lord bless you and keep you;**
> **the Lord make his face to shine upon you**
> **and be gracious unto you;**
> **the Lord lift up his countenance upon you**
> **and give you peace. Amen.**

5 *Any others ready for Confirmation also kneel and the
congregation continues in prayer, the minister saying:*

> Most gracious God and Father,
> you have called us into the service of your kingdom
> and you equip us for the work we have to do.
> Give your servants
> who have professed their faith in you
> the grace of the Holy Spirit
> that they may be strong in faith
> and able to keep the promises
> they have made this day;
> through Jesus Christ our Lord. **Amen.**

6 The Confirmation and Reception

*The minister, laying his hand on the head of each of the
candidates in turn, or raising his hand in blessing over
each, beginning with those just baptized, says:*

> *A ...* The God of all grace,
> who has called you to Christian faith and service,
> confirm and strengthen you with the Holy Spirit
> and keep you faithful to Christ all your days. **Amen.**

Then the candidate(s) standing, the minister says to the congregation:

You are witnesses that A ... (C, E ...) *has* been received into the family and household of God by baptism, and *has* (together with N, P, R ...) been confirmed and admitted to the full privileges and responsibilities of the Church, and in particular to membership of this congregation.

He then says to the new member(s):

In the Name of the Lord Jesus Christ, welcome.

Here the minister and one or more of the elders gives the right hand of fellowship to the new member(s).

May your joining us be a blessing to you and to all of us, and may our one Lord keep us one with all his people, for ever.

7 **Prayer** *follows in these or other words:*

Almighty God we give you thanks
that by the guidance of your Spirit
and through the life and witness of the Church
you bring us to Christ
and enable us to confess our faith in him.
We give you thanks
for your servants whom we have welcomed this day,
for your grace and truth made known to them
and for their commitment to your service.
Uphold and strengthen them in their discipleship;
deepen their understanding of the Gospel
and of the Christian way of life.
Keep them always true to Christ.
Let your blessing rest continually
on the work and witness of this church,
that we who have been called to serve you in this
place, recalling our own baptism,
may now and always be found faithful;
through Jesus Christ our Lord.   **Amen.**

If the Service takes place within the Order of Worship for the Lord's Supper, after the sermon (and a hymn) the foregoing prayer may be joined to, or included within, the Prayers for the Church and the World: or, in those prayers, the minister may say:

We pray for those whom we have now received
into the full privileges and responsibilities
of membership of the Church

and then continue in the prayer as in the Order of Worship for the Lord's Supper.

Confirmation of those already Baptized

This act may precede or follow the prayers for the Church and the world, and so be brought into close relation to prayers, offertory (and communion).

1 Introduction

The minister says:

In the Name of the Lord Jesus Christ, and in accordance with the decision of the Church Meeting, we are now to receive AB, (CD, etc.) into the full privileges and responsibilities of membership of the Church, and in particular into membership of this congregation.

By baptism they were welcomed into the family and household of God, and engaged to be the Lord's. They now come, in response to the call of Christ and the leading of the Holy Spirit, to make their own profession of Christian faith, and to accept for themselves the responsibilities and privileges of membership.

Then let us hear that they profess the Christian Faith and that they intend, in dependence on the help of God, to live as faithful members of the Church and to serve Christ in the world.

2 The Promises

The candidates come forward and, as they stand facing

him, the minister says to them:

A., (and C., etc.) I ask you in the presence of God
and before this congregation,
Do you confess your faith in one God, Father, Son
and Holy Spirit,
taking the Father to be your Father,
the Son to be your Saviour and Lord,
the Spirit to be your Helper and Guide?

I do

Do you promise, in dependence on God's grace,
to be faithful in private and public worship,
to live in the fellowship of the Church and to share in
its work;
and to give and serve, as God enables you, for the
advancement of his kingdom throughout the world?

I do

Do you promise, by that same grace, to follow Christ
and to seek to do and to bear his will all the days of
your life?

I do

And do you trust in his mercy alone to bring you into
the fulness of the life of the world to come?

I do

*Instead of the foregoing questions, a form of declaration
may be used, such as the following:*

**I confess my faith
in one God, Father, Son and Holy Spirit,
taking the Father to be my Father,
the Son to be my Saviour and Lord,
the Spirit to be my Helper and Guide.
I promise,
in dependence on God's grace,**

to be faithful in private and public worship;
to live in the fellowship of the Church
and to share in its work;
and to give and serve, as God enables me,
for the advancement of his kingdom
throughout the world.
I promise, by that same grace,
to follow Christ
and to seek to do and to bear his will
all the days of my life;
and I trust in his mercy alone
to bring me into the fulness
of the life of the world to come.

3 Prayer *follows, the minister saying:*

Let us pray.

Most gracious God and Father
you have called us into the service of your Kingdom
and you equip us for the work we have to do.
Give your servants
who have professed their faith in you
the grace of the Holy Spirit
that they may be strong in faith
and able to keep the promises
they have made this day;
through Jesus Christ our Lord. **Amen.**

4 The Confirmation and Reception

The congregation standing, there follows the Act of Confirmation. The minister, laying his hand on the head of each of the candidates in turn as they stand or kneel, says:

The God of all grace,
who has called you to Christian faith and service,
confirm and strengthen you with the Holy Spirit
and keep you faithful to Christ all your days. **Amen.**

If he has been kneeling, the candidate then stands, and the minister says:

In the Name of the Lord Jesus Christ
I declare you to be admitted to the
full privileges and responsibilities of membership of the Church
and in particular to membership in this congregation.

He then says to the new member(s)

In the Name of the Lord Jesus Christ, welcome.

Here the minister and one or more of the elders give the right hand of fellowship to the new member(s).

May your joining us be a blessing to you and to all of us,
and may our one Lord keep us one with all his people, for ever.
Amen.

5 Prayer *follows, in such words as these:*

Almighty God we give you thanks
that by the guidance of your Spirit
and through the life and witness of the Church
you bring us to Christ
and enable us to confess our faith in him.
We give you thanks
for your servants whom we have welcomed this day,
for your grace and truth made known to them
and for their commitment to your service.
Uphold and strengthen them in their discipleship;
deepen their understanding of the Gospel
and of the Christian way of life.
Keep them always true to Christ.
Let your blessing rest continually
on the work and witness of this church,

that we who have been called to serve you in this
place, re-affirming our own membership vows,
may now and always be found faithful;
through Jesus Christ our Lord. **Amen.**

*If the Service of Confirmation takes place within the
Order of Worship for the Lord's Supper, after the sermon
(and a hymn) the foregoing prayer may be joined to, or
included within, the Prayers for the Church and the
World: or, in those prayers, the minister may say:*

We pray for those whom we have now received
into the full privileges and responsibilities
of membership of the Church

*and then continue in the prayer as in the Order of Worship
for the Lord's Supper.*

Reception of Members from Other Churches

This normally takes place at the Lord's Supper. It precedes the reception of any members on profession of faith.

1 *The minister says*

In the name of the Lord Jesus Christ, and in accordance with the decision of the Church Meeting, we are now to receive into membership of this church, by letter of transfer from ... Church, N... (*or, according to circumstances*, N..., who is a member in good standing with the ... Church).

All stand. The new member may come forward, or the minister may go to him/her.

2 *The minister says*

Let us hear from *him* a declaration that *he* intends, in dependence on the help of God, to live as a faithful member of this fellowship.

N..., do you, confessing anew your faith in one God, Father, Son and Holy Spirit, promise to share with us in the life of this church, and to be faithful in the duties of membership?

I do.

Or,

The minister may say

N... comes to share with us in the life of this church and all the privileges and responsibilities of membership here.

3 *The minister then says*

In the name of the Lord Jesus Christ, welcome.

Here the minister (with or without other representatives of the church) shakes hands with the new member.

May your joining us be a blessing to you and to all of us, and may our one Lord keep us one with all his people, for ever and ever.   **Amen.**

An Act of Thanksgiving for the Birth of a Child
The Dedication of Parents and the Blessing of Children

This Act is intended for parents who are church members and who, on grounds of belief, do not wish to have their children baptized; and also for parents who are not able in conscience to take the vows required at the baptism of infants. The Act is not a substitute for baptism, not is it to be taken as implying a departure by the United Reformed Church from the practice of the baptism of infants.

The Act has been designed to take place at any suitable point within worship. At a pre-arranged time, the parents with their child should take their place at the front of the congregation.

Introduction

1 *The minister says:*

We welcome to this service A and C who have come to give thanks to God for the birth of their child N..., to seek God's blessing upon *him*, and to dedicate themselves (again) to the high task of parenthood.

We share in the parents' thanksgiving. We acknowledge the claim of this child upon the prayers and support of the Church. We welcome *him* as Jesus

64

himself welcomed children. And we affirm that it is the duty of parents and of the Church so to work together that this child may come to know Jesus Christ as Saviour and Lord.

The Word

2 We read in the Old Testament:

Hear, O Israel: The Lord our God is one Lord; and you shall love the Lord your God with all your heart, and with all your soul and with all your might. And these words which I command you this day shall be upon your heart; and you shall teach them diligently to your children, and shall talk of them when you sit in your house, and when you walk by the way, and when you lie down, and when you rise.

Deut. 6: 4–7 (RSV)

Further, we read in the Gospels:

They brought children for Jesus to touch. The disciples rebuked them, but when Jesus saw this he was indignant, and said to them, 'Let the children come to me; do not try to stop them; for the kingdom of God belongs to such as these. I tell you, whoever does not accept the kingdom of God like a child will never enter it'. And he put his arms round them, laid his hands upon them, and blessed them.

Mark 10: 13–16 (NEB)

Thanksgiving, Dedication and Blessing

3 *The minister says*

Let us all stand (*addressing the parents says:*)

Do you thank God for the gift of this child?

We do

C

Do you, as parents, dedicate yourselves to God?

We do

Do you promise, by God's help, to provide a Christian home for this child, and to bring *him* up in the faith of the Gospel and the fellowship of the Church?

We do

Where parents are not members, the third question may take this alternative form:

Do you promise so to order your lives that your child will be surrounded by love and goodness?

We do

May the Lord bless you and give you grace faithfully to carry out these promises.

The minister, or a member of the congregation, says:

We as a congregation, and on behalf of the whole Church of Jesus Christ, undertake to provide, for this child, instruction in the Gospel of God's love, the example of Christian faith and character, and the strong support of the family of God in prayer and friendship.

Then the minister, laying his hand upon the child's head and pronouncing his/her name, says:

Jesus blessed the children.

N... in his name I bless you. The peace of God, Father, Son, and Holy Spirit, be with you, now and always. **Amen.**

and/or

N... the Lord bless you and keep you
The Lord make his face to shine upon you
and be gracious to you;

the Lord lift up his countenance upon you
and give you peace. **Amen.**

The minister says to the parents:

May this child bring you joy. May health, strength
and wisdom be given *him*. And in due time may *he*
come to be baptised, making *his* own profession of
faith and committing *his* life to Christ as *his* Saviour
and Lord.

The minister then says to the congregation:

This child is now commended to you, the congregation, for your prayers and concern.

Prayer

4. *The minister says:*

Let us pray.

O God, the Father of all, from whom every family in
heaven and on earth takes its name, we thank you for
the gift of this child. We thank you for the love that
prepared for *his* coming and welcomed *him* into the
world, and for the great hopes for *his* future which
these parents treasure. Be with them in their home.
Keep them faithful to their promises. Guide them in
the Christian upbringing of their child, and give them
ever deeper knowledge and love of Christ.

Help us all so to act, that they and their family may
find in the Christian fellowship a source of strength
and love.

We commend this child to your fatherly care. Give
him health of body and mind. Bring *him* in due time
to commit *himself* to Christ, so that *he* may faithfully
serve you, and may come, with us, to share the joys of
your eternal kingdom; through Jesus Christ our Lord.
Amen.

Wedding Service

1 *The minister calls the congregation to worship God, saying:*

Let us worship God.

God created mankind in his own image,
male and female he created them;
and God blessed them. *Gen. 1: 27 (Adapted)*

God is love,
and those who live in love, live in God;
and God lives in them. *1 John 4: 16 (Adapted)*

Prayer of Approach

2 *The minister may say:*

Let us pray.

Almighty God
to whom all hearts are open,
all desires known,
and from whom no secrets are hid;
cleanse the thoughts of our hearts
by the inspiration of your Holy Spirit,
that we may perfectly love you,
and worthily magnify your holy Name,
through Christ our Lord. **Amen.**

3 *A hymn or psalm may be sung:*

4 *The congregation may sit, **the bridal party remaining standing**. The bride and bridegroom stand before the minister and he says:*

> We are gathered here in the presence of God
> to celebrate the wedding of AB and CD,
> to rejoice with them,
> and to support them with our prayers.

5 The Purpose of Marriage

Marriage is a gift and calling of God, and is not to be entered upon lightly or thoughtlessly, but reverently and responsibly, in obedience to the Gospel of Christ.

God has provided it for the companionship of help and comfort in mutual care, so that husband and wife may live faithfully together.

God has provided it for the fulfilling of human love in mutual honour, so that husband and wife may know each other with delight.

(God has provided it for the birth and nurture of children, so that they may find the security of love, and grow up in the heritage of faith.)

God has provided it for the enrichment of society, so that husband and wife being joined together may enter into the life of the community as a new creation.

AB and CD now come to give their free consent, and to exchange their vows of faithfulness to each other for the whole of their life together.

6 *The minister says to the congregation:*

> If anyone knows of any reason why they may not
> lawfully be married to each other, let him now
> declare it.

or

> Due notice of their intention has been given, and no
> objection has been made.

The Legal Declarations

7 *Where the law requires it, the minister says to the couple:*

I now ask you both to say that you know of no reason
why you may not lawfully be married:

*The man says in the presence of the Authorised Person (or
the Registrar) and two witnesses, as required by law:*

> **I do solemnly declare
> that I know not
> of any lawful impediment
> why I, AB
> may not be joined in matrimony
> to CD.**

*The woman says, in the presence of the same persons, as
required by law:*

> **I do solemnly declare
> that I know not
> of any lawful impediment
> why I, CD
> may not be joined in matrimony
> to AB.**

*The lessons may be read now and an address given, or they
may be deferred until after the Marriage Blessing.*

Prayer for Sincerity

8 *The minister may say:*

Let us pray.
> Loving Father God
> we ask that as A and C take the vows of marriage
> they may be conscious of your presence with them.
> Help them to be true to each other.

Bless the giving and receiving of the wedding ring(s),
symbol of unending love
and reminder of the vow and covenant made this day.
We ask this for your love's sake. **Amen.**

The congregation may stand to witness the promises.

The Promises

9 *The minister says to the bridegroom:*

A, will you take C to be your wife in Christian
marriage?
Will you love her, comfort her, honour and protect
her, in times of prosperity and health,
and in times of trouble and suffering,
and be faithful to her as long as you both shall live?

I will

The minister says to the bride:

C, will you take A to be your husband in Christian
marriage?
Will you love him, comfort him, honour and protect
him, in times of prosperity and health,
and in times of trouble and suffering,
and be faithful to him as long as you both shall live?

I will.

10 *The minister may say:*

Who gives this woman to be married to this man?
(or Who gives the bride away?)

The father (or friend) of the bride may answer: **I do.**

11 *The bride and bridegroom turn to face each other. The
father of the bride (or the bride's friend) may place her
right hand in that of the bridegroom. The couple's right
hands being joined, the man says to the woman in the
presence of the Authorised Person (or the Registrar) and
two witnesses:*

**I call upon these persons here present
to witness that I, AB
do take thee, CD,
to be my lawful wedded wife***
in accordance with God's holy will
to have and to hold
from this day forward
for better for worse,
for richer for poorer,
in sickness and in health,
to love and to cherish,
till death us do part
and to this end
I pledge my word.

*The woman then says to the man, in the presence of the
same persons:*

**I call upon these persons here present
to witness that I, CD,
do take thee, AB,
to be my lawful wedded husband***
in accordance with God's holy will
to have and to hold
from this day forward,
for better for worse,
for richer for poorer,
in sickness and in health
to love and to cherish
till death us do part,
and to this end
I pledge my word.

**The following shorter form of the legal declaration may
be used when the Authorised Person is present but not
when the Registrar attends:*

**I, AB, do take thee, CD,
to be my wedded wife (or husband).**

The Giving of the Ring(s)

12 *The minister receives the ring(s) and gives it (one) to the bridegroom, who places it on the bride's finger, and holding it there, says:*

I give you this ring in God's name
as a symbol of all that we have promised
and all that we shall share:

The bride may place a ring on the bridegroom's finger, and say the same words, or alternatively when there is only one ring, may say:

I receive this ring in God's name
as a symbol of all that we have promised
and all that we shall share.

The Declaration

13 *The minister joins their right hands together and says to the congregation:*

A and C have declared before God and before you that they will live together in Christian Marriage; they have made sacred promises to each other, and have symbolised their marriage today by joining hands and by the giving and receiving of a ring (rings).

I therefore pronounce them to be husband and wife,
in the name of God, Father, Son and Holy Spirit.
What God has joined together, man must not separate.

The Marriage Blessing

14 *The couple may kneel, and the minister may say:*

May the Lord bless you and take care of you;
May the Lord be kind and gracious to you;
May the Lord look on you with favour
and give you peace.   **Amen.**

And he may add:

Blessed be God the Father
     who gives joy to bridegroom and bride;
Blessed be the Lord Jesus Christ
     who brings new life to mankind;
Blessed be the Holy Spirit of God
     who brings us together in love.
Blessed be Father, Son and Holy Spirit,
     One God to be praised for ever. **Amen.**

15 *A hymn or psalm may be sung.*
(Psalms 121, 23 and 37: 3–7 are suitable)

16 *A selection of readings may be read, if not used earlier—*
the following are suitable:

Genesis 1: 26–28, 31a;	Philippians 1: 9–11;
Song of Songs 8: 6–7a;	Colossians 3: 12–16a, 17;
Tobit 8: 5–9;	1 John 3: 18–24;
Ecclesiasticus 26: 1–4;	1 John 4: 7–13;
Romans 12: 1–2, 9–13;	Matthew 7: 21, 24–27;
1 Corinthians 13: 1–8a, 13;	Mark 10: 6–9;
Ephesians 3: 14–21;	John 2: 1–11;
Ephesians 5: 1–2, 25–33;	John 15: 9–12.

17 *An address may be given, if not given earlier.*

The Prayers

18 *The minister says:*

Let us pray.

*Prayers may be made for Christian Family Life, for the
gift of children, and for concerns outside the family. The
following intercession may be used:*

God our Father,
     you have given A and C grace to see one another
     in the special light of love.

May your love in Christ deepen their love,
 and bring them through life
 bearing each other's burdens
 and sharing each other's joys.

Bless their families and friends;
 May they always thank you for them.

Bless their (new) home;
 May they welcome both friend and stranger to it.
(Bless them in the gift of children;
 May they be loving, wise and caring parents).

Father God,
 we thank you that in our earthly life
 you speak to us of eternal life:

May A and C
 know you more clearly,
 love you more dearly,
 and follow you more nearly,
 day by day;
 through Jesus Christ our Lord. **Amen.**

19 *The Lord's Prayer may be said:*

20 *A hymn may be sung:*

The Blessing

21 *The minister says:*

 May God, the giver of hope,
 fill you with all joy and peace
 because you trust in him,
 so that you may have abundant life,
 through the power of his Holy Spirit.

 The blessing of God Almighty,
 the Father, the Son, and the Holy Spirit,
 be among you,
 and remain with you always. **Amen.**

The Blessing of a Civil Marriage

The following service may be used when a couple have been married in a Registry Office and wish to add a religious ceremony to that solemnisation.

The Service of Blessing of a Civil Marriage in no way supersedes or invalidates any marriage previously solemnised, and record of it should not be entered in a marriage register.

1 *The persons whose marriage is to be blessed stand before the minister in public worship, the husband on the right hand of his wife.*

2 *After a hymn the minister says:*

We are gathered here in the presence of God to ask his blessing on A and C's marriage. Christian marriage is a gift and calling of God, entered in obedience to the Gospel of Christ. Today A and C give thanks for that gift, and acknowledge that calling.

We declare that
God has provided marriage for the companionship of help and comfort in mutual care, so that husband and wife may live faithfully together.

God has provided it for the fulfilling of human love in mutual honour, so that husband and wife may know each other with delight.

(God has provided it for the birth and nurture of children, so that they may find the security of love, and grow up in the heritage of faith.)

God has provided it for the enrichment of society, so
that husband and wife being joined together may
enter into the life of the community as a new creation.

3 Prayer

God our Father
your generous love surrounds us,
and everything we enjoy comes from you.
We confess our ingratitude for your goodness,
and our selfishness in the use of your gifts.
We ask you to forgive us,
and to fill us with true thankfulness,
through Jesus Christ our Saviour.   **Amen.**

O God,
you have taught us through Jesus
that love is the fulfilling of the law.
Grant to your servants,
that, loving one another,
they may continue in your love until their lives' end;
through the same Jesus Christ our Lord.   **Amen.**

4 *One or more lessons may be read. Those listed in the
Wedding Service are suitable. An address may follow the
reading(s).*

The Promise

5 *All stand and the minister says to the husband:*

A., you have taken C. to be your (lawful wedded)
wife.
Since you wish to acknowledge before God your
desire that your married life should be according to
his will,

I ask you, therefore,
will you love her, comfort her, honour and protect
her, in times of prosperity and health,
and in times of trouble and suffering,
and be faithful to her as long as you both shall live?

I will.

The minister then says to the wife:

C., you have taken A. to be your (lawful wedded)
        husband.
Since you wish to acknowledge before God your
desire that your married life should be according to
his will,
I ask you, therefore,
will you love him, comfort him, honour and protect
him, in times of prosperity and health,
and in times of trouble and suffering,
and be faithful to him as long as you both shall live?

I will.

The Blessing

6 *The husband and wife kneel and the minister says:*

God the Father give you joy.
God the Son give you new life.
God the Holy Spirit unite you.

The Lord bless you and watch over you;
The Lord make his face shine upon you and be
        gracious to you;
the Lord look kindly on you and give you peace.

May the One God,
        present with you now,
        keep you true to each other.

May the ring(s) you wear
> be the symbol(s) of unending love,
> and reminder of the covenant made this day.

May you love and cherish each other
> till death parts you.

And to God be the praise for ever.   **Amen.**

7 *The couple stand, join their right hands, and the minister says:*

Those whom God has joined together,
> man must not separate.

8 *A hymn may be sung.*

9 *The service may continue with prayers for the couple, for Christian Family life, for the gift of children, and for concerns outside the family, and with the Lord's Prayer.*

10 *The service may conclude with the Lord's Supper from the offertory, or with a hymn and a dismissal and blessing.*

Service Before a Funeral

This order may be used when a service is requested at the home of the deceased, or if the body is brought into church some time before the funeral.

Scripture Sentences

1 *A selection from the following should be used:*

> I am the resurrection and the life, says the Lord; he who believes in me, though he die, yet shall he live, and whoever lives and believes in me shall never die.
>
> *John 11: 25–26 (RSV)*

> God is our refuge and strength, a very present help in trouble.
>
> *Psalm 46: 1 (RSV)*

> Praise be to the God and Father of our Lord Jesus Christ, the all-merciful Father, the God whose consolation never fails us! He comforts us in all our troubles, so that we in turn may be able to comfort others in any trouble of theirs and to share with them the consolation we ourselves receive from God.
>
> *2 Corinthians 1: 3, 4 (NEB)*

> Praise be to the God and Father of our Lord Jesus Christ who in his great mercy gave us a new birth into a living hope by the resurrection of Jesus Christ from the dead.
>
> *1 Peter 1: 3, 4 (NEB)*

Prayer of Approach

2 Let us pray

> Eternal God,
> Lord of life, conqueror of death,
> our help in every time of trouble,
> comfort us who mourn;
> and give us grace, in the presence of death,
> to worship you, the ever-living,
> so that we may have sure hope of eternal life
> and be enabled to put our whole trust
> in your goodness and mercy:
> through Jesus Christ our Lord.   **Amen.**

Readings

3 *A selection from the following may be used*

> The Lord is my light and my salvation;
>   whom then shall I fear?
> The Lord is the stronghold of my life;
>   of whom shall I be afraid?
> When the wicked, even my enemies and my foes,
>   come upon me to devour me,
> they shall stumble and fall.
> If an army encamp against me,
>   my heart shall not be afraid:
> and if war should rise against me,
>   yet will I trust.
> One thing I have asked from the Lord
>   which I will require:
> that I may dwell in the house of the Lord
>   all the days of my life,
> To see the fair beauty of the Lord,
> and to seek his will in his temple.
> For he will hide me under his shelter in the day of
>   trouble,
> and conceal me in the shadow of his tent,
>   and set me high upon a rock.

And now he will lift up my head
above my enemies round about me.
And I will offer sacrifices in his sanctuary with
    exultation:
I will sing, I will sing praises to the Lord.

Psalm 27: 1–8
(The Psalms, A new translation for Worship.)

O Lord, you have searched me out and known me:
you know when I sit or when I stand,
    you comprehend my thoughts long before.
You discern my path and the places where I rest:
you are acquainted with all my ways.
For there is not a word on my tongue
but you, Lord, know it altogether.
You have encompassed me behind and before
and have laid your hand upon me.
Such knowledge is too wonderful for me,
so high that I cannot endure it.
Where shall I go from your spirit
or where shall I flee from your presence?
If I ascend into heaven, you are there:
if I make my bed in the grave you are there also.
If I spread out my wings towards the morning,
or dwell in the uttermost parts of the sea,
even there your hand shall lead me,
and your right hand shall hold me.
If I say 'Surely the darkness will cover me and the
    night will enclose me,'
the darkness is no darkness with you,
    but the night is as clear as the day:
the darkness and light are both alike.
How deep are your thoughts to me, O God,
and how great is the sum of them!
Were I to count them,
    they are more in number than the sand.

Were I to come to the end,
    I would still be with you.

Psalm 139: 1–11, 17–18
(The Psalms, A new translation for Worship.)

Let not your heart be troubled: ye believe in God,
believe also in me. In my Father's house are many
mansions: if it were not so, I would have told you. I
go to prepare a place for you. And if I go and prepare
a place for you, I will come again and receive you
unto myself; that, where I am, there ye may be also.
And whither I go ye know, and the way ye know.
Thomas saith unto him, Lord, we do not know
whither thou goest; and how can we know the way?
Jesus saith unto him, I am the way, the truth, and the
life: no man cometh unto the Father but by me.

I will not leave you comfortless: I will come to you.
Yet a little while, and the world seeth me no more;
but ye see me: because I live, ye shall live also. Peace
I leave with you, my peace I give unto you: not as the
world giveth, give I unto you. Let not your heart be
troubled, neither let it be afraid.

John 14: 1–6, 18–19, 27 (AV)

What shall we then say to these things? If God be for
us, who can be against us? He that spared not his own
Son, but delivered him up for us all, how shall he not
with him also freely give us all things? Who shall lay
anything to the charge of God's elect? It is God that
justifieth. Who is he that condemneth? It is Christ
that died, yea rather, that is risen again, who is even
at the right hand of God, who also maketh
intercession for us. Who shall separate us from the
love of Christ? Shall tribulation, or distress, or
persecution, or famine, or nakedness, or peril, or
sword?

Nay, in all these things we are more than conquerors through him that loved us. For I am persuaded, that neither death, nor life, nor angels, nor principalities, nor powers, nor things present, nor things to come, nor height, nor depth, nor any other creature, shall be able to separate us from the love of God, which is in Christ Jesus our Lord.

Romans 8: 31–35, 37–39 (AV)

Prayers of Thanksgiving and Petition

4 *These, or other prayers, may be used:*

Loving God, Lord of Life and Death, we praise you that all people are made in your image and held under your care, we praise you that we are made to need each other's love and so reflect your truth and life. We thank you for the life of N... for the love and mercy he/she received from you and gave to us. Above all we rejoice in the gift of your love we see in Jesus Christ. Give us the confidence to believe that as he has conquered death, nothing can separate us from your love. We ask that we may at last share with N... the completeness of your eternal Kingdom, through Jesus Christ our Lord. **Amen.**

Almighty God, Father of all mercies and giver of all comfort, deal graciously, we pray, with those who mourn, that, casting all their care on you, they may know the consolation of your love; through Jesus Christ our Lord. **Amen.**

5 The Lord's Prayer

6 The grace of our Lord Jesus Christ,
    and the love of God,
      and the fellowship of the Holy Spirit, be with you
        all. **Amen.**

Funeral Service

Approach

Scripture Sentences

A selection from the following should be used:

I am the resurrection and the life, says the Lord; he
who believes in me, though he die, yet shall he live,
and whoever lives and believes in me shall never die.

John 11: 25–26 (RSV)

The eternal God is your dwelling-place, and under-
neath are the everlasting arms.

Deut. 33: 27 (RSV)

Cast your burden on the Lord, and he will sustain
you.

Psalm 55: 22 (RSV)

God is our refuge and strength, a very present help
in trouble.

Psalm 46: 1 (RSV)

In his favour is life; weeping may endure for a night,
but joy cometh in the morning.

Psalm 30: 5 (AV)

Blessed are those who mourn, for they shall be
comforted.

Matt. 5: 4 (RSV)

God so loved the world that he gave his only son, that whoever believes in him should not perish but have eternal life.

John 3: 16 (RSV)

I am sure that neither death nor life, nor angels, nor principalities, nor things present, nor things to come, nor powers, nor height nor depth, nor anything else in all creation, will be able to separate us from the love of God in Christ Jesus our Lord.

Rom. 8: 38, 39 (RSV)

Now we see in a mirror dimly, but then face to face. Now I know in part; then I shall understand fully, even as I have been fully understood.

1 Cor. 13: 12 (RSV)

Praise be to the God and Father of our Lord Jesus Christ, the all-merciful Father, the God whose consolation never fails us! He comforts us in all our troubles, so that we in turn may be able to comfort others in any trouble of theirs and to share with them the consolation we ourselves receive from God.

2 Cor. 1: 3, 4 (NEB)

Praise be to the God and Father of our Lord Jesus Christ, who in his great mercy gave us new birth into a living hope by the resurrection of Jesus Christ from the dead!

1 Peter 1: 3, 4 (NEB)

Alternatively the minister may use this preface, or one of his own devising:

We have come together to worship God; to give him thanks and praise for the life of N... whose days among us have now drawn to a close; and to share our grief over one loved and respected by those who knew *him*, and one whose love and concern for us have been till now a strengthening.

And we meet in the faith that death is not the ultimate calamity that it seems, and that we can be enabled to face it without fear, or bitterness, or guilt.

Praise be to the God and Father of our Lord Jesus Christ, who in his great mercy gave us new birth into a living hope by the resurrection of Jesus Christ from the dead.

Jesus said: 'Let not your hearts be troubled, neither let them be afraid.'

Prayers

Then may follow one of these prayers:

Eternal God, the creator and upholder of all things, your ways are not as our ways, nor your thoughts as our thoughts; your wisdom is unsearchable; your purposes cannot fail. Humbly we worship you, and as trusting children we come to you, the Father of our Lord Jesus Christ and our Father. Let not our hearts be troubled, neither let us be afraid.

Comfort us in the natural grief of parting, and help us to bear ourselves as Christian men and women, for whom death itself is swallowed up in victory; through Jesus Christ our Lord. **Amen.**

God our Father, our refuge and strength, a helper close at hand in time of trouble: you can change the shadow of death into the brightness of a new morning. We turn to you now, and to your Word, so that we may renew our trust and our hope, and be lifted from darkness and distress into the light and peace of your presence: through Jesus Christ our Lord. **Amen.**

Heavenly Father, in your son Jesus Christ you have given us a true faith and a sure hope. Strengthen this faith and hope in us now and all our days. Help us to believe in the communion of saints, the forgiveness of

sins, and the resurrection to eternal life; through Jesus
Christ our Lord. **Amen.**

Gracious Lord, enable us to listen lovingly for your
word. May we console each other with the message
you proclaim, so finding light in darkness and faith in
the midst of doubt; through Jesus Christ our
Lord. **Amen.**

The Promises of God

Psalms

*One of the following psalms may be read, or said
responsively:*

The Lord is my shepherd;
>I shall not want.
He maketh me to lie down in green pastures;
>he leadeth me beside the still waters.
He restoreth my soul;
>he leadeth me in the paths of righteousness for
>his name's sake.
Yea, though I walk through the valley of the shadow
of death,
I will fear no evil;
>for thou art with me; thy rod and thy staff they
>comfort me.
Thou preparest a table before me in the presence of
mine enemies;
>thou anointest my head with oil; my cup runneth
>over.
Surely goodness and mercy shall follow me all the
days of my life;
>and I will dwell in the house of the Lord for
>ever.

Psalm 23 (AV)

The Lord is merciful and gracious,
  slow to anger, and plenteous in mercy.
He will not always chide;
  neither will he keep his anger for ever.
He hath not dealt with us after our sins;
  nor rewarded us according to our iniquities.
For as the heaven is high above the earth,
  so great is his mercy toward them that fear him.
As far as the east is from the west,
  so far hath he removed our transgressions from
    us.
Like as a father pitieth his children,
  so the Lord pitieth them that fear him.
For he knoweth our frame;
  he remembereth that we are dust.
As for man, his days are as grass;
  as a flower of the field, so he flourisheth.
For the wind passeth over it, and it is gone;
  and the place thereof shall know it no more.
But the mercy of the Lord is from everlasting to
    everlasting upon them that fear him,
  and his righteousness unto children's children;
To such as keep his covenant,
  and to those that remember his commandments
    to do them.

Psalm 103: 8–18 (AV)

I will lift up mine eyes unto the hills,
  from whence cometh my help.
My help cometh from the Lord,
  which made heaven and earth.
He will not suffer thy foot to be moved:
  he that keepeth thee will not slumber.
Behold, he that keepeth Israel
  shall neither slumber nor sleep.
The Lord is thy keeper:
  the Lord is thy shade upon thy right hand.

The sun shall not smite thee by day,
nor the moon by night.
The Lord shall preserve thee from all evil;
he shall preserve thy soul.
The Lord shall preserve thy going out and thy
coming in
from this time forth, and even for evermore.

*Psalm 121 (A*ᴠ

The following Psalms or Psalm portions are also suitable:

Psalms 39: 4–8, 12; 42; 90: 1–6, 10, 12; 130.

4 New Testament Readings

One or more of the following passages may be read:

The Spirit of God joins with our spirit in testifying
that we are God's children; and, if children, then
heirs. We are God's heirs and Christ's fellow-heirs, if
we share his sufferings now in order to share his
splendour hereafter. For I reckon that the sufferings
we now endure bear no comparison with the splendour, as yet unrevealed, which is in store for us.

And in everything, as we know, the Spirit co-operates
for good with those who love God and are called
according to his purpose.

With all this in mind, what are we to say? If God is
on our side, who is against us? He did not spare his
own Son, but surrendered him for us all; and with
this gift how can he fail to lavish upon us all he has to
give? Who will be the accuser of God's chosen ones?
It is God who pronounces acquittal: then who can
condemn? It is Christ—Christ who died, and, more
than that, was raised from the dead—who is at God's
right hand, and indeed pleads our cause. Then what
can separate us from the love of Christ? Can affliction
or hardship? Can persecution, hunger, nakedness,

peril, or the sword? In spite of all, overwhelming victory is ours through him who loved us. For I am convinced that there is nothing in death or life, in the realm of spirits or superhuman powers, in the world as it is or the world as it shall be, in the forces of the universe, in heights or depths—nothing in all creation that can separate us from the love of God in Christ Jesus our Lord.

Romans 8: 16–18, 28, 31–35, 37–39 (NEB)

If it is for this life only that Christ has given us hope, we of all men are most to be pitied. But the truth is, Christ was raised to life—the first fruits of the harvest of the dead. For since it was a man who brought death into the world, a man also brought resurrection of the dead. As in Adam all men die, so in Christ all will be brought to life; but each in his own proper place: Christ the first fruits, and afterwards, at his coming, those who belong to Christ. Then comes the end, when he delivers up the kingdom to God the Father, after abolishing every kind of domination, authority, and power. For he is destined to reign until God has put all enemies under his feet; and the last enemy to be abolished is death.

But, you may ask, how are the dead raised? In what kind of body? A senseless question! The seed you sow does not come to life unless it has first died; and what you sow is not the body that shall be, but a naked grain, perhaps of wheat, or of some other kind; and God clothes it with the body of his choice, each seed with its own particular body.

So it is with the resurrection of the dead. What is sown in the earth as a perishable thing is raised imperishable. Sown in humiliation, it is raised in glory; sown in weakness, it is raised in power; sown as an animal body, it is raised as a spiritual body. If there is such a thing as an animal body, there is also a spiritual body.

What I mean, my brothers, is this: flesh and blood can never possess the kingdom of God, and the perishable cannot possess immortality.

This perishable being must be clothed with the imperishable, and what is mortal must be clothed with immortality. And when our mortality has been clothed with immortality, then the saying of Scripture will come true: 'Death is swallowed up; victory is won!' 'O Death, where is your victory? O Death, where is your sting?' The sting of death is sin, and sin gains its power from the law; but, God be praised, he gives us the victory through our Lord Jesus Christ. Therefore, my beloved brothers, stand firm and immovable, and work for the Lord always, work without limit, since you know that in the Lord your labour cannot be lost.
1 Corinthians 15: 19–26, 35–38, 42–44, 50, 53–58 (NEB)

Then I saw a new heaven and a new earth, for the first heaven and the first earth had vanished, and there was no longer any sea. I saw the holy city, new Jerusalem, coming down out of heaven from God, made ready like a bride adorned for her husband. I heard a loud voice proclaiming from the throne: 'Now at last God has his dwelling among men! He will dwell among them and they shall be his people, and God himself will be with them. He will wipe away every tear from their eyes; there shall be an end to death, and to mourning and crying and pain; for the old order has passed away!'

Then he who sat on the throne said, 'Behold! I am making all things new!' And he said to me, 'Write this down; for these words are trustworthy and true. Indeed', he said, 'they are already fulfilled. For I am the Alpha and the Omega, the beginning and the end. A draught from the water-springs of life will be my free gift to the thirsty. All this is the victor's heritage; and I will be his God and he shall be my son.'
Revelation 21: 1–7 (NEB)

'Set your troubled hearts at rest. Trust in God always; trust also in me. There are many dwelling-places in my Father's house; if it were not so, I should have told you; for I am going there on purpose to prepare a place for you. And if I go and prepare a place for you, I shall come again and receive you to myself, so that where I am you may be also; and my way there is known to you.' Thomas said, 'Lord, we do not know where you are going, so how can we know the way?' Jesus replied, 'I am the way; I am the truth and I am life; no one comes to the Father except by me.

'I will not leave you bereft; I am coming back to you. In a little while the world will see me no longer, but you will see me; because I live, you too will live.

'Peace is my parting gift to you, my own peace, such as the world cannot give. Set your troubled hearts at rest, and banish your fears.'

John 14: 1–6, 18–19, 27 (NEB)

The following passages are also suitable:

Wisdom 4: 7–15 *Jerusalem Bible* (for premature death);
Rom. 14: 7–12; 2 Cor. 4: 7–18; 2 Cor. 5: 1–10;
1 Thess. 5: 1–11; 1 Peter 1: 3–9;
Rev. 7: 9–17; Rev. 22: 1–5; John 6: 35–40.

An address or sermon may be given.

Prayers

One prayer may be taken from each group.

Thanksgiving for the Victory of Christ

God, our Father, we thank you that you sent your Son Jesus Christ to die for us and rise again. His cross declares your love to be without limit; his resurrection, that death, our last enemy, is doomed. By his victory we are assured of the promise that you will never leave us or forsake us; that neither death nor life, nor things present nor things to come, can separate us from your love in Christ Jesus our Lord. **Amen.**

Gracious God, whose purpose for all men is one of good, from whose love nothing can separate us, neither death nor life, nor things present nor things to come, we offer you our thanks and praise for all that you have done for the family of man through Jesus Christ. By giving him to live and die for us, you have made known your ways with men and women, and shown that your love has no limit. By raising him from the dead, you have promised that those who trust in him will share his resurrection-life. Grant us, then, that confidence in you, which, even in the hour of deep distress and great perplexity, clings to your guiding hand and finds strength and comfort: through Jesus Christ our Lord.   **Amen.**

7 Commendation of the departed

Eternal God, before whose face the generations rise and pass away: we praise you for all your servants departed this life in your faith and love, especially for N... whom today we commend into your sure keeping; each recalling in a moment of silence what *he* has meant to *his* loved ones, friends and colleagues....

We give thanks for all your goodness towards *him*; all *he* accomplished by your grace; and all that *he* was to those who loved *him*. And now we praise you that for *him* sorrow and sickness are ended, death itself is past, and *he* lives for ever in your love and care; through Jesus Christ our Lord.   **Amen.**

Almighty and Eternal God, we give thanks for the witness of your faithful people in all generations. Especially now we lift up our hearts in gratitude for the life of N... whom we commit into your care and keeping; for the gracious memories *he* has left behind ... *(here may follow appropriate thanksgivings)*...for everything in *his* life that reflected your goodness and love. Help us to believe that death is the gateway to a fuller life and that *he* is safe in your keeping; through Jesus Christ our Lord. **Amen.**

Heavenly Father, by your mighty power you gave us life, and in your love you have given us new life in Jesus Christ. We now entrust N... to your merciful keeping: in the faith of Christ Jesus your Son our Lord, who died and rose again to save us, and is now alive and reigns with you and the Holy Spirit in glory for ever. **Amen.**

Petition

For all who mourn:

Almighty God, Father of all mercies and giver of all comfort: deal graciously, we pray, with those who mourn, that, casting all their care on you, they may know the consolation of your love; through Jesus Christ our Lord. **Amen.**

Gracious God, our heavenly Father, sustain and comfort those beset by grief and sorrow. Be their refuge and strength, a very present help in trouble. May they know the love that passes understanding—the love of him who by death has conquered death, and by rising again has opened the gates of everlasting life, Jesus Christ our Lord. **Amen.**

For ourselves:

Almighty God, we pray that, encouraged by the example of your saints, we may run with patience the race that is set before us, looking to Jesus, the pioneer and perfecter of our faith; so that at the last we may join those whom we love in your presence where there is fullness of joy; through Jesus Christ our Lord. **Amen.**

Father, do not let grief overwhelm your children but rather teach us how to live out our lives serenely and gently with others, following the good example of those now at rest; and may we at the last enter with them into the fullness of your unending joy; through Jesus Christ our Lord. **Amen.**

Almighty God, in this hour of sorrow we confess our sins to you. In the vigour of life we often live as though our destinies were in our own control and not in yours. Forgive us, O Father: help us to walk more humbly with you, doing your will with diligence and faithfulness; looking to that day when we shall be gathered with all those who love you, in your eternal kingdom of light and joy; through Jesus Christ our Lord. **Amen.**

9 *The* **Lord's Prayer** *may then be said.*

10 *Where the committal is to be in another place, this part of the service may end with a hymn, and an ascription of glory, such as:*

Now to the One who can keep you from falling
and set you in the presence of his glory,
jubilant and above reproach,
to the only God our Saviour,
be glory and majesty, might and authority,
through Jesus Christ our Lord,
before all time, now, and for evermore. **Amen.**

Jude 24, 25 (NEB)

The Committal

11 *One or more of the following sentences may be said at the grave or at the crematorium, prior to the words of committal:*

> Jesus says: 'I am resurrection and I am life. If a man has faith in me, even though he die, he shall come to life; and no one who is alive and has faith shall ever die.'
>
> *John 11: 25–26 (NEB)*

> If we live, we live for the Lord; and if we die, we die for the Lord. Whether therefore we live or die, we belong to the Lord.
>
> *Rom. 14: 8 (NEB)*

> The Lord says: 'Do not be afraid, I am the first and the last, and I am the living one; for I was dead and now I am alive for evermore, and I hold the keys of death and death's domain.'
>
> *Rev. 1: 17b–18 (NEB)*

Then shall follow the words of committal.

> Having entrusted our *brother* (*or N...*) into the hands of God, we now commit *his* mortal body to the ground (*or* to be cremated*) in sure and certain hope of the resurrection to eternal life through our Lord Jesus Christ, who died, was buried, and rose again for us. To him be glory for ever. **Amen.**

or

> Seeing that the earthly life of our *brother* has come to an end, we commit *his* body to be buried (cremated*), confident of the resurrection to eternal life through our Lord Jesus Christ. **Amen.**

> *(earth to earth), ashes to ashes, dust to dust... may be added.*

D

or

Having commended into God's hands our *brother*
departed, we commit *his* body to the ground (*or* to be
cremated*); putting our whole trust and confidence in
the mercy of our Heavenly Father, and in the victory
of his Son, Jesus Christ our Lord, who died, was
buried and rose again for us, and lives and reigns for
ever. **Amen.**

> *(earth to earth), ashes to ashes,
> dust to dust... *may be added.*

12 *Then may be said:*

Thou wilt show me the path of life:
in thy presence is fullness of joy;
at thy right hand there are pleasures for evermore.

Psalm 16: 11 (AV)

or

He will wipe away every tear from their eyes, and
death shall be no more, neither shall there be mourning nor crying nor pain any more, for the former
things have passed away.

Rev. 21: 4 (RSV)

or

They shall never again feel hunger or thirst, the sun
shall not beat on them nor any scorching heat, because the Lamb who is at the heart of the throne will
be their shepherd and will guide them to the springs
of the water of life; and God will wipe away all tears
from their eyes.

Rev. 7: 16–17 (NEB)

or

You, Christ, are the king of glory,
the eternal Son of the Father.
When you became man to set us free
you did not spurn the Virgin's womb.
You overcame the sting of death,
and opened the kingdom of heaven to all believers.
You are seated at God's right hand in glory.

We believe that you will come, and be our judge.
    Come then, Lord, and help your people,
    bought with the price of your own blood,
    and bring us with your saints
    to glory everlasting.

TE DEUM part ii
(International Consultation on English Texts)

13 *Then shall be said one of the following (or similar) prayers and the blessing:*

Save your people, Lord, and bless your inheritance.
Govern and uphold them now and always.
Day by day we bless you.
We praise your name for ever.
Keep us today, Lord, from all sin.
Have mercy on us, Lord, have mercy.
Lord, show us your love and mercy;
for we put our trust in you.
In you, Lord, is our hope:
and we shall never hope in vain.

TE DEUM part iii
(International Consultation on English Texts)

Almighty God, you have bound together all your people in heaven and on earth in one holy fellowship: let not our thoughts linger here, but help us to believe that your servant's life has made a new beginning, with your mercy and your love still around *him*.

Strengthened by this assurance, may we return to the duties which await us in the world, resolved to be more faithful to you and more helpful to one another, for the sake of those no longer with us upon earth; through Jesus Christ our Lord. **Amen.**

14   The peace of God, which passes all understanding, keep your hearts and minds in the knowledge and love of God and of his son, Jesus Christ our Lord.

And the blessing of God almighty, the Father, the
Son, and the Holy Spirit,
be among you,
and remain with you always. **Amen.**

Funeral Service for a Child

Approach

1 Scripture Sentences

As a father pities his children,
so the Lord pities those who fear him.
Psalm 103: 13 (RSV)

As one whom his mother comforts,
so will I comfort you, says the Lord.
Isaiah 66: 13 (RSV)

He shall feed his flock like a shepherd,
he will gather the lambs in his arms, and
he will carry them in his bosom.
Isaiah 40: 11a (RSV)

Jesus says, I am the good shepherd.
The good shepherd lays down his life for the sheep.
My sheep hear my voice, and I know them,
and they follow me; and I give them eternal life,
and they shall never perish, and no one shall snatch
them out of my hand.
My Father, who has given them to me, is greater than
all, and no one is able to snatch them out of the
Father's hand.
John 10: 11, 27–29 (RSV)

Alternatively, the minister may use this preface, or one of his own devising:

We have come together to worship God; to thank him for his love, and to remember the life of N... to share our grief over the loss of this child and commend *him/her* into the eternal care of God.

We meet in the faith that death is not the end and that we can be enabled to face it without fear, or desperation, or guilt.

2 *Psalm 23 is said or sung*

3 Prayer of Approach

Eternal God, Father of us all
Whose love knows no end;
Please help us, through this service
to know that you are close to us.
As we hear your promises
help us to believe them
and accept the comfort they offer.
Let our faith be deepened even through our loss
so that we may be spared bitterness, doubt or
unending sorrow and find your lasting peace.
We ask this through Jesus Christ our Lord.   **Amen.**

The Promises of God

4 Psalms

The following Psalms or Psalm portions are suitable.

Psalm 121; 39: 4–8, 12; 42; 90: 1–6, 10, 12; 130.

5 New Testament Readings

One or more of the following passages is read:

And they were bringing children to him, that he might touch them; and the disciples rebuked them. But

when Jesus saw it he was indignant, and said to them;
'Let the children come to me, do not hinder them; for
to such belongs the kingdom of God. Truly, I say to
you, whoever does not receive the kingdom of God
like a child shall not enter it.' And he took them in his
arms and blessed them, laying his hands upon them.

Mark 10: 13–16 (RSV)

Jesus said; 'Let not your hearts be troubled; believe in
God, believe also in me. In my Father's house are
many rooms; if it were not so, would I have told you
that I go to prepare a place for you? And when I go
and prepare a place for you, I will come again and
will take you to myself, that where I am you may go
also. I am the way, and the truth, and the life; no one
comes to the Father, but by me. Peace I leave with
you; my peace I give to you; not as the world gives do
I give to you. Let not your hearts be troubled, neither
let them be afraid.'

John 14: 1–3, 6, 27 (RSV)

Blessed be the God and Father of our Lord Jesus
Christ, the Father of mercies and God of all comfort,
who comforts us in all our affliction, so that we may
be able to comfort those who are in any affliction,
with the comfort with which we ourselves are
comforted by God. For as we share abundantly in
Christ's sufferings, so through Christ we share
abundantly in comfort too.

2 Cor. 1: 3–5 (RSV)

6 *An Address may be given*

Prayers

7 Prayer of Thanksgiving

Gracious God,
your purpose for all your children is one of good;
from your love nothing can separate us,
neither death nor life,
nor things present, nor things to come.

We thank you for all you have done
for the family of man through Jesus Christ.
By giving him to live and die for us,
you have made known your ways with us,
you have shown that your love has no limit.
By raising him from the dead,
you have promised that those who trust in him
will share his resurrection-life.
Grant us, then, that confidence in you
which, even at the time of our distress and
        bewilderment,
clings to your guiding hand and
so finds strength and comfort.
We thank you for the love and joy
N . . . brought with *him/her*
and called out from us.
We commend *him/her* into your
safe, eternal keeping;
through Jesus Christ our Lord.   **Amen.**

8 The Lord's Prayer

9 [*Where the Committal is to be in another place, this part
of the service may end with a hymn, and an ascription of
glory, such as:*

Now to the One who can keep you from falling
and set you in the presence of his glory,
jubilant and above reproach, to the only God our
        Saviour,
be glory and majesty, might and authority,
through Jesus Christ our Lord,
before all time, now, and for evermore.   **Amen.**]

The Committal

10   We have commended N... to God's loving care; now we commit *his/her* body to be cremated/or to the ground in the certain hope of eternal life, through our Lord Jesus Christ. **Amen.**

I am sure that neither death, nor life, nor things present, nor things to come, nor height, nor depth, nor anything else in all creation, will be able to separate us from the love of God in Christ Jesus our Lord.

Romans 8: 39–39 (RSV)

The Lamb in the midst of the throne will be their shepherd, and he will guide them to springs of living water; and God will wipe away every tear from their eyes.

Revelation 7: 17 (RSV)

11 Prayer of Petition

Loving Father, whose Son is the resurrection and the life, give us the confidence that you have received N... into your peace.

Let us too rest in that peace and look for your purpose being fulfilled now and in the future. Remind us day by day that in everything, you work for good with those who love you. Help us now to live our lives within your love and peace until at last we are united with all your children in the happiness of your eternal kingdom: through Jesus Christ our Lord. **Amen.**

12 The Blessing

The peace of God, which passes all understanding, keep your hearts and minds in the knowledge and love of God and of his son, Jesus Christ our Lord. And the blessing of God almighty, the Father, the Son, and the Holy Spirit, be among you, and remain with you always. **Amen.**

D*

Service for
the Burial or Scattering of Ashes

1 Scripture Sentences

God loved the world so much that he gave his only
Son, that everyone who has faith in him may not die
but have eternal life.

John 3: 16 (NEB)

We believe that Jesus died and rose again; and so it
will be for those who died as Christians; God will
bring them to life with Jesus. Thus we shall always be
with the Lord. Console one another, then, with these
words.

1 Thess. 4: 14, 17b, 18 (NEB)

If we live, we live for the Lord; and if we die, we die
for the Lord. Whether therefore we live or die, we
belong to the Lord.

Rom. 14: 8 (NEB)

2 Reading

No wonder we do not lose heart! Though our outward
humanity is in decay, yet day by day we are inwardly
renewed. Our troubles are slight and short-lived; and
their outcome an eternal glory which outweighs them
far. Meanwhile our eyes are fixed, not on the things
that are seen, but on the things that are unseen: for
what is seen passes away; what is unseen is eternal.
For we know that if the earthly frame that houses us

today should be demolished, we possess a building which God has provided—a house not made by human hands, eternal, and in heaven.

2 Cor. 4: 16–5: 1 (NEB)

3 The Burial or Scattering takes place

We have entrusted N... to God's eternal keeping. Now we commit *his/her* ashes to their resting-place; in the sure and certain hope of resurrection to eternal life through our Lord Jesus Christ, who died, was buried, and rose again for us. To him be glory for ever. **Amen.**

4 Prayer of Petition

This or another prayer may be used.

Eternal God, who destroyed death's power over us by your Son's death and resurrection, we remember N... with love and thankfulness, and ask that *he/she* and all who have believed in you may share your eternal life and peace. Confirm us in the belief that death is the gateway to a fuller life and that *he/she* is safe in your keeping: through Jesus Christ our Lord. **Amen.**

5 The Blessing

The peace of God, which passes all understanding, keep your hearts and minds in the knowledge and love of God and of his son, Jesus Christ our Lord.

And the blessing of God almighty, the Father, the Son, and the Holy Spirit, be among you, and remain with you always. **Amen.**

Ordination and Induction of Ministers

Preliminary Note

The Basis of Union states that it is part of Function (ii) of the District Council '... with the Moderator of Synod or his deputy presiding, to conduct, in fellowship with the local church, any ordinations and/or inductions of ministers within the district.' (The Manual, 1973, page 23.)

Since 'presiding' and 'conducting' are so nearly the same, it is implicit that on these occasions the Moderator of Synod acts as the chief representative of the District Council, of which he is a member. It also follows that if for any reason the Moderator of Synod cannot preside, his deputy will normally be the District Chairman.

It is the responsibility of the District Council to make the arrangements for the service. In order to give body to the fact that it is the whole District Council which, through the person of the presiding Moderator, is conducting the service, it is recommended that every ordination/induction should be a duly constituted and minuted meeting of the District Council, and that wherever practicable the representatives of the District Council, both ministerial and lay, should gather beforehand, together with others taking part in the service, in order that the Moderator or his deputy may constitute the meeting. The questions of whether the ministerial representatives should robe, and whether the District Council representatives should enter the church as a body (and, if so, whether they should form part of the procession with the 'platform party' or enter slightly beforehand) should be resolved ad hoc. *But they should be resolved, not left to chance: and the situation should be avoided where the District Council's lay representatives take their places beforehand while the ministers, robed or otherwise, enter with the platform party.*

The District Chairman may constitute the District Council in the presence of the congregation and then invite the Moderator to preside.

The Approach to God

1 *The call to worship may be responsive.*

President:
  Let us worship God.

(If not already standing, all stand now.)

  Christ is the head of his body, the church:
  he is the source of the body's life;
  he is the firstborn Son who was raised from death,
  in order that he alone might have the first place
  in all things.

Congregation:

  **Through the Son, God decided
  to bring the whole universe back to himself.**

President:

  Glorify the Lord with me,

Congregation:

  And let us exalt his name together.

President:

  Enter his gates with thanksgiving
  and his courts with praise.

Congregation:

Give thanks to him and bless his name.

2 *A hymn may follow here or after the first of the following prayers.*

3 *President:*

Let us pray.
> We praise and adore you, God our Father.
>> You are the maker of everything
>> and because of your will
>> all things came to be and continue in being.

> We praise and adore you, Jesus Christ.
>> You are the Word made flesh.
>> Through you we come to the Father
>> and have joy in his presence.

> We praise and adore you, Holy Spirit.
>> You are the Father's gift to men,
>> and because of your ceaseless activity
>> the church is continually renewed in its
>> mission to the world.

> With the whole church on earth and in heaven
> we praise and adore you, Father, Son and Holy Spirit,
>> for the greatness of your power,
>> the wideness of your mercy,
>> and the wisdom of your purpose for mankind.

> Glory to you, our God, for ever.   **Amen.**

President:
> Let us make confession of sin (saying together . . .).

President (or President and Congregation together):

> God, our Father, you have called us to be united to
>> Christ and to be limbs and organs of his body.

We confess with shame our failure, as his members, to
    carry out his will.

Blind, lazy and divided your church has been,
    claiming the keys of the kingdom
    but not using them properly.

We have made people think the door is shut
    that you went to such pains to open.

We have separated what you had joined in Christ—
    spirit and matter,
    sacred and secular.

We have loved those who loved us, and let it stop
    there.

Forgive us. Renew us. Enlighten and strengthen us.

May our bearing towards one another
    arise out of our life in Christ:
    and may that life enhance
    the life of the whole world.

For the sake of Jesus Christ our Lord.

*(If the prayer has been spoken by the President alone, the
congregation here responds* **'Amen'**.*)*

President:

God of life and power,
we open our hearts and rejoice
that the depth of your being is love.
We praise you for showing us in Jesus
what you call us to be.
Come in the power of your Spirit
to bind us together and make us your own
to the glory of Christ our Lord.   **Amen.**

The Ministry of the Word

4 *President:*

In the name of the Lord Jesus Christ, the king and

head of the church, who has ascended on high and has given gifts for building up his body, we have met here to ordain AB to the ministry of the Word and Sacraments and to induct *him* to serve in this pastorate/team ministry/chaplaincy/etc.

(*Or, at the induction of one already ordained, he says:*

In the name of the Lord Jesus Christ, the king and head of the church, who has ascended on high and has given gifts for building up his body, we have met here to induct AB to this pastorate/team ministry/ chaplaincy/etc., and to pray for *him* in the work God is calling *him* to do.)

Let us therefore first listen for the word of God in the Scriptures as they are read and preached.

5 *Scripture reading follows, including always a passage from the New Testament. The following recommendations are made with the New English Bible particularly in mind.*

Old Testament
Exodus 33: 12–16a; Deuteronomy 30: 11–20; 1 Kings 19: 1–21; Nehemiah 8: 1–12; Isaiah 6: 1–8; Isaiah 49: 1–6; Isaiah 52: 7–10; Isaiah 55: 1–13; Isaiah 61: 1–4.

New Testament
Matthew 5: 1–12; Mark 3: 13–19; Mark 6: 31–44; Mark 10: 35–45; Luke 4: 14–21; Luke 10: 1–11; John 13: 1–17; John 15: 1–17; Acts 20: 17–38; Romans 10: 6–15; Romans 12: 1–21; 1 Corinthians 12: 4–13; 2 Corinthians 4: 1–15; Ephesians 3: 8–21; Ephesians 4: 1–16; Phillippians 2: 1–15; 1 Peter 4: 10–11; 5: 1–4.

6 *A hymn should be sung before the sermon. If there are two readings the hymn may come between them.*

7 Sermon. (*This may take the form of a brief 'contemporizing' of the Scriptures read. If it is thought of as a charge, to minister or church or both, it should avoid covering the same ground as the Affirmations below, or the ordination/induction prayer, and in this case may be given after the Act of Ordination/Induction.*)

The Act of Ordination/Induction

8 *The Interim Moderator (or comparable representative person) now introduces the minister-elect to the President, relating briefly, as appropriate, the circumstances of the former's call to the ministry and to the instant situation. The minister-elect may make a personal statement.*

9 *President:*

We believe that God gives the grace and authority for the office and work to which anyone is called. He does so in answer to the prayers of the church. We act and speak as part of the one, holy, catholic and apostolic church, and in the faith which it proclaims.

A statement concerning the Nature, Faith and Order of the United Reformed Church *is read as follows, or in another approved form:*

The United Reformed Church confesses the faith of the Church Catholic in one God, Father, Son and Holy Spirit.

The United Reformed Church acknowledges that the life of faith to which it is called is a gift of the Holy Spirit continually received in Word and Sacrament and in the common life of God's people.

The United Reformed Church acknowledges the Word of God in the Old and New Testaments, discerned under the guidance of the Holy Spirit, as the supreme authority for the faith and conduct of all God's people.

The United Reformed Church accepts with thanksgiving the witness borne to the Catholic faith by the Apostles' and Nicene Creeds, and recognises as its own particular heritage the formulations and declarations of faith which have been prepared from time to time by Congregationalists and Presbyterians, in which they have stated the gospel and sought to make its implications clear.

The United Reformed Church testifies to its faith, and orders its life, according to the Basis of Union, believing it to embody the essential notes of the Church Catholic and Reformed. The United Reformed Church nevertheless reserves its right and declares its readiness at any time to alter, add to, modify or supersede this Basis so that its life may accord more nearly with the mind of Christ.

The United Reformed Church under the authority of Holy Scripture and in corporate responsibility to Jesus Christ its everliving head, acknowledges its duty to be open at all times to the leading of the Holy Spirit and therefore affirms its right to make such new declarations of its faith and for such purposes as may from time to time be required by obedience to the same Spirit.

The United Reformed Church, believing that it is through the freedom of the Spirit that Jesus Christ holds his people in the fellowship of the One Body, upholds the rights of personal conviction. It shall be for the Church, in safeguarding the substance of the faith and maintaining the unity of the fellowship, to determine when these rights are asserted to the injury of its unity and peace.

The United Reformed Church declares that the Lord Jesus Christ, the only king and head of the Church, has herein appointed a government distinct from civil government and in things spiritual not subordinate thereto, and that civil authorities, being always subject to the rule of God, ought to respect the rights of conscience and of religious belief and to serve God's will of justice and peace for all men.

The United Reformed Church declares its intention, in fellowship with all the Churches, to pray and work for such visible unity of the whole Church as Christ wills and in the way he wills, in order that men and nations may be led more and more to glorify the Father in heaven.

10 Affirmations

The presiding minister shall say to the minister-elect immediately after the reading of the Statement:

AB do you undertake to exercise your ministry in conformity with this statement?

I do.

He shall then ask:

Do you confess anew your faith in one God, Father, Son and Holy Spirit?

I do.

Do you believe that the Word of God in the Old and New Testaments, discerned under the guidance of the Holy Spirit, is the supreme authority for the faith and conduct of all God's people?

I do.

Do you believe that Jesus Christ, born into this world, living as a man among men, dying upon the cross, raised from the dead and reigning for evermore, is God's gift of himself to the world whereby his love and mercy are revealed, offering to all men forgiveness, reconciliation and eternal life? And will you faithfully proclaim this gospel?

This I believe and this I will proclaim.

Do you believe that the Church is God's people, gathered by his love to serve him in reconciling the world to himself?

I do

Are zeal for the glory of God, love for the Lord Jesus Christ and a desire for the salvation of men, so far as you know your own heart, the chief motives which lead you to enter this ministry?
(At induction to a new charge, the question shall end 'to enter on the duties of the ministry in this place'.)

They are.

Do you promise to fulfil the duties of your charge with all fidelity, to lead your people in worship, to preach the Word and administer the Sacraments, to exercise pastoral care and oversight, and to give leadership to the Church in its mission to the world?

I do.

Do you promise to live a holy life and always to maintain the truth of the gospel, whatever trouble or persecution may arise?

I do.

Do you promise as a minister of this Church to seek its purity, peace and true prosperity, to cherish brotherly love towards all other Churches and to endeavour always to build up the one, holy, catholic and apostolic Church?

I do.

And all these things do you profess and promise as the Lord Jesus Christ shall give you grace and strength to fulfil the same?

I do.

1 *Then the President invites all present to stand, and the people of the place to answer the following questions:*

President:

Do you recognize the calling of AB to be a Christian minister and receive *him* as from God to serve among you here?

People: **We do.**

President:

Do you promise to pray for AB and for each other, to share with *him* in seeking and doing the will of God, and to give *him* due honour, consideration and encouragement, building one another up in faith, hope and love?

People: **We do.**

2 *A hymn is sung. The 'Veni Creator Spiritus', or similar hymn of invocation, e.g. Congregational Praise 269 = Revised Church Hymnary 241 = Church Hymnary, Third Edition 117, or New Church Praise 102, would be suitable.*
It is suggested that all except the minister-elect (who kneels, though at an induction only he need not) remain standing for the prayer which follows.

3 *A form for ordination is first given, followed by the modification necessary when induction only is taking place. It is urged that these forms should be consulted even if not used as they stand.*

President:

Let us pray.

Lord God our Father, we thank you for your love
        towards us.

We thank you for calling us to be your people,
    dedicated to proclaim the power and grace of
      your Son
    and to rejoice in his salvation.

We thank you for the many abilities you give,
    to equip your people for work in your service
    and to build up the body of Christ.

Those appointed now lay their hands on the ordinand's head.

IN YOUR NAME
AND IN OBEDIENCE TO YOUR WILL
WE NOW ORDAIN *AB*
TO BE A MINISTER IN YOUR CHURCH.
ENRICH *HIM* WITH THE HOLY SPIRIT:
GIVE *HIM* GRACE TO BE FAITHFUL IN *HIS*
    WORK.

Impart to *him* wisdom, understanding and power to allow your Word free course among the people. May your voice be heard in *his* preaching and your hand be seen in *his* administering of Baptism and the Lord's Supper. Enable *him* so to care for the young, comfort the troubled and sorrowful, and listen to the needs of all, that the church may be strengthened in faith and friendship. Make *him* ready to learn as well as to teach, to receive as well as to give. May *he* so reinforce the church in its witness and service that it may be a caring, reconciling and prophetic community in this neighbourhood. Sustain *him* through the temptations and testing of frustration, misunderstanding and success. Bless *him* in *his* home. (Give to *his* family patience with the demands made upon *him* and joy in their own contribution to *his* ministry.)

Give grace to this congregation/community/etc., that they, receiving A (*Christian name only*) as their minister called and chosen through the working of your Holy Spirit, may respond to *his* service among them and with one heart and mind work together for the furtherance of the gospel.

Through Jesus Christ our Lord, who lives and rules with you, Father, and the Holy Spirit, one God, world without end.

Congregation: **Amen.**

When induction only is taking place, the opening of the prayer can be the same as that above. Omitting the laying-on of hands it may then continue:

'We ask you to renew in your servant AB the gifts of your Holy Spirit as *he* begins *his* ministry in this place/situation/etc. Give to *him* wisdom...' (*and so on, as above*).

All now standing, the President makes the declaration of ordination and/or induction, as follows:

President:

In the name of the Lord Jesus Christ, and as the representative of the ———— District Council acting on behalf of the United Reformed Church in England and Wales, I declare AB to be

ordained to the ministry of the Word and Sacraments in the Church of Jesus Christ, and to be inducted to the pastorate of this congregation/chaplaincy/etc.	inducted to the pastorate of this congregation/chaplaincy/ etc.

May the God of peace, who brought up from the dead our Lord Jesus, the great Shepherd of the sheep, by the blood of the eternal covenant, make you perfect in all goodness so that you may do his will; and may he make us what he would have us be through Jesus Christ, to whom be glory for ever and ever.

Congregation: **Amen.**

15 (*A Bible may be presented to the new minister, with some such words as these:*

We present to you this Bible.
Here are the words of eternal life.
Build up God's people in his truth,
    and serve them in his name.)

16 (*The right hand of fellowship may be given by the President and others appointed.*)

17 *A hymn is sung.*

18 Prayers of Intercession

(*The Lord's Prayer may conclude these: or, if Communion is to follow, it may be deferred until the end of the prayer of thanksgiving there.*)

19 *Hymn.* (*The Lord's Supper may follow at this point.*)

20 Dismissal

(*It is fitting that the President should complete the service by pronouncing the blessing.*)

(*At the close of the service, the District Council's representatives should follow the platform party out of the church, and when all are assembled the President may close the meeting of the District Council with some such words as these:*

Into your hands, our Father, we commend
our gathering and our intention,
our action and our hope:
through Jesus Christ our Lord.   **Amen.**)

Ordination and Induction of Elders

The ordination and induction of elders takes place when the local church meets for worship. The minister or Interim-moderator of the church presides. It is appropriate that ordinations be held in the context of the Sacrament of the Lord's Supper. The elders and elders-elect take their appointed places.

The Ministry of the Word

1 *The Call to Worship and Prayer of Approach.*

2 *A hymn may follow here or after the first prayers.*

3 *Prayers of Adoration, Confession, and for Pardon or an Assurance of Pardon.*

4 *The following prayer of Supplication may be used here or at another appropriate point:*

Lord God, you give us many gifts,
that we may share them
in the work of your Church.
Help us to receive gladly
and to give generously,
that with all your people
we may know the wonder of your love
and be faithful in service;
through Jesus Christ our Lord. **Amen.**

5 *The minister says here, or before the Preface*

In the name of the Lord Jesus Christ, the king and head of the Church, who has ascended on high and has given gifts for building up his body, we are today to ordain AB, CD ... to the eldership of the United Reformed Church, and to induct him/her/them together with NO, PQ ... to the eldership in this church.

6 *Scripture Readings, including always a passage from the New Testament, should be read. They may be appropriate to the day or special lessons may be chosen, the following being suitable:*

Old Testament

Exodus 18: 13–27; Numbers 11: 16, 17, 24–30; Isaiah 42: 1–9; Ezekiel 34: 11–16.

New Testament

Matthew 25: 14–28; Mark 10: 35–45; Luke 12: 35–40; John 4: 31–38; John 10: 1–6, 10b–18; John 21: 15–17; Acts 20: 28–35; Romans 12: 1–18; 1 Corinthians 3: 5–11; 1 Corinthians 12: 4–13; Philippians 2: 1–3; Ephesians 4: 1–16; 1 Peter 4: 7–11; 1 Peter 5: 1–4.

7 *A psalm or hymn may be sung between two lessons, or before the sermon.*

8 *The Sermon may be an exposition of the scriptures read. If it is thought of primarily as a charge to elders or church or both, it should avoid covering the same ground as the Affirmations or the ordination/induction prayer, and in this case may be given after the Act of Ordination/Induction.*

9 *A Creed or The Statement of Faith of the United Reformed Church, or a Credal Hymn or the Te Deum may be used after the sermon.*

Act of Ordination/Induction

Preface

10 *The minister says:*

The Lord Jesus Christ continues his ministry in
and through the Church, the whole people of God
called and committed to his service. To equip them
for this ministry he gives particular gifts, and calls
some of his servants to exercise them in offices duly
recognised within the Church. Some are called to
the ministry of Word and Sacraments; some are
called to be elders.

Elders share with the minister in the pastoral
oversight and leadership of the local church. To
each is normally entrusted a group of members. In
the Elders' Meeting they take counsel together for
the whole congregation. They are responsible for
making provision for Christian worship and
education, for maintaining proper standards of
membership, and for promoting witness and service
to the community, mission at home and abroad, and
the peace, unity and welfare of the Church. It is
their duty to arrange for the proper maintenance of
church buildings, and to ensure the oversight of
church finances. Some elders represent the local
church in the wider councils of the Church, and by
virtue of their membership of these councils
represent the whole Church to the local church.

Elders, being elected by the Church Meeting, are
ordained to their office and inducted to serve for
such period as the church which elects them
determines. Their ordination and induction is an act
of the Church, and it is right at this time to make a
public declaration of the nature, faith and order of
the United Reformed Church, and identify
ourselves with it.

A Statement concerning the Nature, Faith and Order of the United Reformed Church is read (see page 113).

Affirmations by the Elders-Elect

The minister then says to the elders-elect, who stand:

In the light of this statement of the nature, faith and order of the United Reformed Church and concerning the functions of eldership, the elders-elect are now to answer the following questions:

Do you confess again your faith in one God, Father, Son and Holy Spirit?

I do.

In dependence on God's grace do you reaffirm your trust in Jesus Christ as Saviour and Lord, and your promise to follow him and to seek to do and to bear his will all the days of your life?

I do.

Do you believe that the Word of God in the Old and New Testaments discerned under the guidance of the Holy Spirit, is the supreme authority for the faith and conduct of all God's people?

I do.

Do you accept the office of elder in the United Reformed Church in this congregation and do you promise to perform the duties of eldership faithfully?

I do.

Affirmations by the church

13 *The minister then asks the people to stand, and says:*

I now call on you, the members of this congregation, to dedicate yourselves anew to Christ and to the task of ministry which he lays on us all, and to promise your support to the new elders in their work.

In answer to three questions will you please answer **'We do'**.

Do you confess again your faith in Jesus Christ as Saviour and Lord?

We do.

Do you seek to fulfil together your common calling to the glory of the one God, Father, Son and Holy Spirit?

We do.

Do you promise to give these elders, whom you have elected to share in the pastoral oversight of this church, your support and encouragement in the Lord?

We do.

14 *Hymn of the Holy Spirit*

Ordination Prayer

15 *The words printed in capitals may be said for each one, the minister naming him/her and, normally with two or more elders, laying hands on his/her head, or they may be said once only, using the names of all being ordained. If the service is one of induction only of elders already ordained, the words in capitals will not be used, but the rest of the prayer can easily be adapted for the purpose.*

Almighty God our Father,
you have set your church in the world
to bear witness to the gospel
and you equip it with those gifts which it needs.

We thank you that now,
in this place,
you have given us men and women
of faith and integrity
and have called them to your service.

IN YOUR NAME
AND IN OBEDIENCE TO YOUR WILL
WE NOW ORDAIN *A.B.*, *C.D.*,...
TO BE (AN) ELDER(S) IN YOUR CHURCH.
ENRICH *HIM* WITH THE HOLY SPIRIT:
GIVE *HIM* GRACE
TO BE FAITHFUL
IN *HIS* WORK.

Grant *him* (and *him* whom we induct into this office)
          the vision and the courage to lead this church
          in its Christian witness in the world.
Make them wise in counsel as those who have the
          mind of Christ;
Accept them as they give themselves to the work of
          your kingdom;
Deepen their knowledge of the truth as it is in Jesus;
And sustain them in care for those committed to their
          charge; through Jesus Christ our
          Lord. **Amen.**

Declaration of Ordination and/or Induction

*The minister says to (each of) those being ordained and/or
inducted:*

A (C and E . . .),
In the name of the Lord Jesus Christ, the only head
          of the Church,

and in accordance with the decision of this church,
I declare you to be ordained to the eldership;
and I induct you (together with N (P and R . . .) into
the office of elder in this church,
in token of which I/we give you the right hand of
fellowship.
The almighty God and Father grant you his grace,
that in this your charge you may be found
faithful.

*If Inductions only are taking place, or if he wishes to make
a separate declaration of those being inducted only, the
minister says:*

N (P and R . . .)
In the name of the Lord Jesus Christ the only head of
the Church,
and in accordance with the decision of this church,
I induct you into the office of elder in this church, in
token of which I/we give you the right hand of
fellowship.
The almighty God and Father grant you his grace
that in this your charge you may be found
faithful.

17 *The right hand of fellowship may also be given by the
existing elders, or by one or more elders on their behalf.*

18 *A hymn may be sung.*

19 *Here may follow the prayers of Intercession, the offertory
and the Communion.*

20 *The service ends with a hymn and a dismissal and blessing.*

Commissioning of a Missionary for Service Overseas

The Commissioning of a missionary takes place at a service convened by the District Council (where possible in the church from which the missionary comes), in the presence of representatives appointed by the Council for World Mission, the Provincial Synod and the District Council. The Chairman of the District Council, or the Provincial Moderator, presides.

The Order of Worship may follow that to which the particular church is accustomed. It should begin with Call to Worship and include Scripture Reading(s), Prayer(s), Hymn(s) and Sermon or Charge. Passages which may be appropriate for Scripture reading are:

Old Testament:
Ruth 1: 8–17; Isaiah 42: 1–9; Isaiah 52: 7–12; Jeremiah 1: 4–10; Ezekiel 3: 16–21; Jonah 3 and 4.

New Testament:
Matthew 9: 35–10: 15; Matthew 28: 16–20; Luke 10: 1–11; John 10: 1–16; John 13: 1–17; John 15: 1–17; John 21: 15–17; Romans 10: 6–17; Romans 12: 1–8; 2 Corinthians 4: 1–7; 2 Timothy 3: 14–4: 5.

The Commissioning

1 *President*

We are today to commission AB for work overseas with the Council for World Mission within the ... Church.

We first identify ourselves with a Statement of our Church concerning its Commitment to World Mission.

The United Reformed Church confesses its faith that the fulness of Christ's Gospel is to be proclaimed to all mankind.

The United Reformed Church acknowledges its responsibility to share in Christ's mission to the whole world through the fellowship of Churches in other lands, giving and receiving help within this fellowship as opportunity offers.

The United Reformed Church rejoices that there are those from its own membership who respond to Christ's call to them to serve him overseas.

The United Reformed Church accepts special responsibility for those of its members whom it recognises and commissions to serve in other churches through the Council for World Mission and accords them a place in its own councils.

Description of the Call

2 *A representative of the Council for World Mission or other suitable person gives a description of the call and the Church (and institution) to which AB is to go and the nature of the particular work which he/she is to undertake.*

The Affirmations *(all standing)*

3 *The President says to the missionary*

Do you confess anew your faith in one God, Father, Son and Holy Spirit?

I do.

Do you believe that he has called you to the work of
the Church overseas?

I do.

The President says to the congregation

Do you, as representing the churches within this
District and in the name of the United Reformed
Church, undertake to support A ... with interest and
prayer?

We do.

The Commissioning Prayer

4 *This prayer, or other suitable prayers, may be used*

Most merciful God and Father,
you have set your Church in the world
to bear witness to the gospel,
and you equip it with the gifts it needs.
We thank you that now, in this place,
you have given us living proof
of the way you call men and women
into new realms of service.

As in your name
we commission N...
for service as a missionary in your church,
we pray that you will enrich him/her with the Holy
      Spirit.
Give him/her grace to be faithful in his/her work.
Lead him/her into an ever deeper understanding of
      the gospel,
and sustain his/her sense of calling to proclaim it.
Through this ministry
reconcile men and women to yourself
and bring them to Christian maturity.

Glory to you for ever!   **Amen.**

Declaration

5 *The president to missionary*

AB, the United Reformed Church recognizes you as a missionary of the Church, called of God and appointed by the Council for World Mission at the invitation of the Church in ... to work with that Church. In the name of the Lord of the Church we commission you and send you forth; and we undertake to continue to share in this world mission with you by our prayers, our money, and our witness.

Here a copy of the Bible may be presented

Go, (live agreeably to this Word and) publish the Gospel of Jesus Christ according to your gifts, calling and abilities as a fellow-worker with the Church in .....

May God bless you and keep you and make you a channel for his grace to the people to whom you are sent. **Amen.**

6 *Representatives of the Council for World Mission, Provincial Synod, District Council and local church shake hands, as a sign of commendation and support, with the missionary (and his wife/her husband).*

The missionary may make a Statement if he/she so wishes.

7 *After the Commissioning the service may continue with a charge to the missionary and to the church, with Prayers of Intercession and Dedication, and with the Lord's Supper if it is to be celebrated; it concludes with a Doxology or hymn of praise and the dismissal and blessing.*

Commissioning of an accredited Lay Preacher

The commissioning of a lay preacher by the District Council (after accreditation by that Council) may take place either at an ordinary meeting of the District Council or at a Communion Service in the lay preacher's own church when appointed representatives of the District Council are present.

The Service may begin with Call to Worship, Hymn(s), Prayer, Scripture Reading(s) and Sermon or Charge. There should in any case be Scripture Reading. Suitable passages are:

Old Testament
Numbers 11: 16–17, 24–30; Isaiah 52: 7–12; Jeremiah 23: 16–22; Ezekiel 3: 16–21.

New Testament
Matthew 9: 53–10: 15; Luke 10: 1–20; Matthew 28: 16–20; John 15: 1–17; Acts 11: 19–26; Romans 1: 8–17; Romans 10: 5–17; 2 Corinthians 5: 11–6: 2.

Preface

1 *The President says:*

The Lord Jesus Christ continues his ministry in and through the Church, the whole people of God called and committed to his service. As equipment for this ministry he gives particular gifts, and calls some of his servants to exercise them in offices duly recognised within his Church.

Among the offices so recognised by the United Reformed Church is that of lay preacher. In order that it may be clearly seen that the worship of the local church is an expression of the worship of the whole people of God, it is for the United Reformed Church to provide for the training and, through District Councils, for the accrediting and commissioning as lay preachers of suitable men and women among its members. These combine with membership of their own church a share in maintaining a regular ministry of the Word in other churches.

We meet to commission as (a) lay preacher(s) AB, CD,... who *has* been accredited by the ... District Council. Let us therefore ask *him* to affirm *his* faith and intention as *he* enter(s) upon this ministry.

The Affirmations

2 *The President says to the Lay Preacher(s)-elect*

Do you·confess again your faith in one God, Father, Son and Holy Spirit?

I do.

In dependence on God's grace do you reaffirm your trust in Jesus Christ as Saviour and Lord and your promise to follow him and to seek to do and to bear his will all the days of your life?

I do.

Do you believe that the Word of God in the Old and New Testaments, discerned under the guidance of the

Holy Spirit, is the supreme authority for the faith and conduct of all God's people?

I do.

Do you believe that you are called to preach the gospel of God's love and mercy to mankind revealed in Jesus Christ?

I do.

Do you undertake to exercise your ministry in accordance with the nature, faith and order of the United Reformed Church and, where this is called for, to participate in team-ministry with workers from this and other branches of the Church?

I do.

(*To the congregation*).

Do you, the members of this (church and) District Council accept AB, CD, EF, ... as (an) accredited lay preacher(s) and promise *him* prayerful support and encouragement in this work?

We do.

3 *Prayer is offered as follows or in some comparable form:*

Most merciful God and Father, you have set your Church in the world to bear witness to the gospel, and you equip it with the gifts it needs.

We thank you that now, in this place, you have given us living proof of the way you call men and women into new realms of service.

As in your name we commission A, C, E, ... to the office of lay preacher in your Church, we pray that you will enrich *him* with the Holy Spirit.

Give *him* grace to be faithful in *his* work.

Lead *him* ever deeper into understanding of the gospel, and sustain *his* sense of calling to proclaim it.

Through this ministry, may men and women be
reconciled to yourself and become mature in Christ.
In his name we pray.   **Amen.**

Declaration of Commissioning

4 *The President says*

In the name of the Lord Jesus Christ the only Head
of the Church

And in accordance with the decision of the District
Council

I declare you to be commissioned to the office of
lay preacher in the United Reformed Church

In token of which I give you the right hand of
fellowship.

5 *The Service may conclude with further prayer, hymn(s)
and blessing or may continue with Communion.*

Induction of a Provincial Moderator

The Induction shall take place in the context of public worship, which though complete need not be long. This form of service is intended for use within the Province to which the Provincial Moderator is to be inducted.

If the Induction takes place within the General Assembly, it is suggested that the Act of Induction should be used as part of one of the Assembly's acts of worship.

The Service shall be conducted by the Moderator of the General Assembly, or his deputy, who shall be accompanied by a Commission of Assembly.

1 *Call to Worship.*

2 *Prayer of Invocation.*

3 *Hymn.*

4 *Prayers of Confession and Supplication.*

5 *The reading of Scripture.*

6 *Hymn of the Holy Spirit.*

7 *The Moderator shall make a statement on the purpose of the Service, and thereafter call upon the Synod Clerk to read the Statement concerning the Nature, Faith and Order of the United Reformed Church.*

8 *The Moderator shall call upon the Provincial Moderator-elect to make the Affirmations.*

9 *The Moderator, having called the congregation to stand, shall address to it this question:*

> Do you the representatives of the churches in this Province acknowledge and receive *N* ... as Moderator of this Synod? And do you promise to encourage and strengthen *him* in *his* ministry, and give *him* all due honour, loyalty and support in the Lord?
>
> **We do.**

10 *The Moderator shall offer prayer, concluding with the Lord's Prayer.*

11 *Thereafter he shall formally declare the Provincial Moderator inducted:*

> In the name of the Lord Jesus, the only head of the Church, I declare you to be inducted to this office and in the name of the Assembly (and of this Province) I give you the right hand of fellowship and bid you God-speed in all your work.

12 *Representatives of the Province (e.g. the Synod Clerk) and of the District Councils may also give the right hand of fellowship.*

13 *Hymn*

14 *Charge to the Provincial Moderator and Province*

15 *Hymn*

16 *Prayers of Thanksgiving and Intercession*

17 *Hymn*

18 *Blessing*

Order of Service
for Healing

INTRODUCTION

Services for Healing are of various kinds:

(a) Sometimes one of the regular Sunday services in church (especially in the evening) is given a particular emphasis.

(b) Sometimes a special healing service is held in church at some other time on a Sunday or on a weekday.

(c) Sometimes a healing service is held in the home of a sick person. This may include Holy Communion.

Sunday Services

Some churches have found it a valuable means of widening the interest and understanding of the healing ministry of the Church if, from time to time, Sunday worship emphasises this aspect of the Church's ministry. This practice is commended to ministers and church meetings for their consideration.

Special Services

For services of the type (b) some parts of the suggested order, not specifically related to healing, could be omitted. Where services are held on church premises it is important that the worship centre is, as far as

possible, helpful to worship in general and the aims of
the healing service in particular. A small congregation
should worship in a side chapel or a small room, rather
than feel lost in a large church.

Services in the home

For services of the type (c) that include Holy
Communion, it is recommended that an elder or some
other church member known to the sick person is
present.

Healing services, in whatever form they are advertised,
should be clearly stated as open to all and not restricted
to those who desire healing for themselves or those
known to them.

Services for healing will vary in their content and order,
according to local circumstances. The order of service
set out contains elements which have proved helpful and
which it is hoped will serve as a guide to those who are
responsible for arranging and conducting healing
services. Adequate time for silent meditation should be
provided, since healing services are essentially services
of waiting upon God.

Where the Laying on of Hands is included it is
recommended that it should be carefully introduced to
avoid misunderstanding, given not only by the minister
but also by others participating in the service as an
indication that this ministry is not restricted to any one
person but is part of the work of the whole Church
seeking wholeness for people. There is nothing magical
about this service; it is carried out in response to the
New Testament promise of healing through Jesus
Christ.

Prayer group

A prayer group is an invaluable part of the healing
ministry in the local church and can also provide the

nucleus for healing services. Where these are held regularly it is recommended that a book be provided into which names of people requesting prayers may be written. Those who are listed should be visited and reports given at subsequent services.

The healing ministry

Worshippers should be reminded that healing was an integral part of the ministry of Christ and that the early Church understood that it was called to continue this ministry as a part of its concern for the welfare of the whole person. Down the centuries God has used a variety of means to bring salvation and healing—through the Church and medical and caring agencies in the world. The Church, through corporate worship and fellowship, and through the individual service of its members, makes known God's love and performs its role as a healing community.

Answered Prayer

Christians believe that God hears and answers prayer but cannot prejudge how he will act in any given situation. Some will find healing, others will receive grace sufficient to face continued suffering, and death will sometimes be seen as an act of divine deliverance. We should offer our worship to God at all times believing, expecting, knowing that God wills our highest good.

Some Practical Suggestions

(a) *Welcome and notices:*
The minister (or leader) should explain that the service is one of praise and openness to God. As worshippers make their requests known to God, so he will make known his will to them.

(b) *Prayers*

(i) Responsive prayers are a valuable means of involving the congregation. Where they are used the responses may be duplicated and handed out with the hymn book.

(ii) The names of those who have asked for prayer may be mentioned during the intercessions.

(iii) Meditation. The minister should explain the procedure to be followed. It might be suggested, for instance, that the congregation meditate upon the Bible reading or sermon. Alternatively, a theme may be chosen with short passages of scripture followed by periods of silence. The silences should be long enough for worshippers to think through the ideas in a passage but not too long as to cause them difficulty.

(c) *The Laying on of Hands*

For ease of administration, people wishing to receive the laying on of hands should be asked to come and sit in the front pew, or a row of chairs can be specially arranged to give those officiating freedom to stand in front of, or behind, the seated persons. Kneeling can be difficult for some, though provision should be made for those who wish to kneel.

After the invitation to come forward is given, a hymn may be sung or an organ voluntary played whilst those wishing the laying on of hands move to their places.

Laying on of hands is customarily given by placing the hands upon the head of each person, so women should be asked to remove their hats. While the hands are placed on the head a prayer is said aloud enabling the whole congregation to share in the prayer for this particular person.

If the minister is leading the service he may arrange for one or two people to assist him in the laying on of hands. The arrangement should be made in good time before the service to allow for the preparation and training of those who will take part.

(d) *Time*

The length of the service is an important consideration. It should take into account for whom the service is being held i.e. for a sick person in bed, or for those who come to a service for healing in church. Worshippers with arthritis cannot sit for too long. Some may find difficulty in kneeling for prayer or the laying on of hands.

Service for Healing

The Order of Service is a guide. Every act of public worship and all services arranged by the Church will always serve in some way to help people who are ill. This Order particularly emphasises our desire to be made well, and suggests where and how the Church might follow Jesus in the 'Laying on of Hands'.

1 Welcome and Notices

The minister shall briefly explain the purpose of the service.

2 Call to Worship

How good it is to give thanks to the Lord, to sing in your honour, Most High God, to proclaim your constant love every morning, and your faithfulness every night. Jesus said: Whoever believes in me will do the works I do—Yes; he will do even greater ones, because I am going to the Father. And I will do whatever you ask in my name.

3 Prayer of Approach

Father God, Creator of the universe and fashioner

of men and women in your image, we worship and adore you.

Lord Jesus, Saviour of the world and friend of each one of us, we worship and adore you.

Holy Spirit, life of the Church and comforter of the needy, we worship and adore you.

One God, you are constantly bringing us fellowship and blessing; help us to open our hearts and lives to your coming in this time of worship. **Amen.**

4 Hymn

5 Prayers of Confession

We confess to you Lord, what we are:
>we are not the people we like others to think we are;
>we are afraid to admit even to ourselves what lies in the depths of our souls.

But we do not want to hide our true selves from you.

We believe that you know us as we are, and yet you love us.

Help us to know and accept ourselves; give us the courage to put our trust in your forgiveness, through Christ our Saviour. **Amen.**

SILENCE for a personal confession of sin

or

Lord God, we confess:
>we have forgotten you and failed in our relationships with others;
>we have been fearful about ourselves and anxious about the future;
>we have spoken hard and bitter words;
>we have been boastful of our achievements and envious of the success of others;
>we have selfishly pursued our own ends and given little time or thought for the needs of others.

Creator and Father, you have made us to live in
harmony and fellowship with you and each other; we
have become divided within and separated from the
source of our strength and joy through our failure to
seek you regularly in prayer.

Lord of our life and our helper at all times, forgive us
and enable us to forgive others, in the name of Christ
our Saviour. **Amen.**

6 Assurance of Pardon

Here are words you may trust, words that merit full
acceptance:
    'Christ Jesus came into the world to save sinners'.
To all who confess their sins and resolve to lead a
new life He says:
    'Your sins are forgiven',
and He also says:
    'Follow me'.
Now to the King of all worlds, immortal, invisible,
the only wise God, be honour and glory for ever and
ever. **Amen.**

7 The Proclamation of the Word of God

*Reading of Scripture and any other appropriate reading by
which God's goodness, mercy and caring concern for his
people are set forth.*

8 Prayers of Thanksgiving

Lord God, accept our thanks for everything that
speaks to us of your love, enriches our lives and gives
purpose to our days.

We give thanks for the world of nature, providing
for our bodily needs; for home and family life in
which we share so much happiness and find your love
made real; for daily work and tasks to do, and the
satisfaction which comes from those well done.

We give thanks for the coming of your Son to live our life and to give us his victory over sin and death. For his teaching, preaching and healing whereby he declared your Fatherhood revealing your power to save those who put their trust in you, we give thanks and praise. For his Church in every age we praise your name, thanking you for those who have handed down to us such a rich heritage of Christian witness and service. May we in our day continue steadfast, courageous and true to our ever living Lord, that men and women everywhere may rejoice to see your power at work in us; through Jesus Christ our Lord. **Amen.**

9 Sermon

10 Silent Meditation—*during which worshippers are invited to meditate on the readings and the sermon.*

11 Hymn

12 Offering and Dedication

13 Prayers of Intercession

Lord God, we ask you to hear us as we bring before you in prayer the needs of others.

We pray for the Church, its life and work:
Lord of the Church, we rejoice in your cross, and ask that your sacrificial love may become the example of all your followers. May your constant presence be our inspiration and power to overcome evil, your Gospel become the hope of all peoples.

We pray for the sick, and all in need of healing:
Father of us all, we rejoice in your creating and providential love, and ask that you will heal the sick, comfort the sorrowing, and reassure the

anxious and despairing. Give them peace, and the
knowledge that none is outside your love and care.
Hear our prayer for our friends who are sick and
for all who have requested our prayers, especially
those whom we now name...

We pray for those who work for the wellbeing and
healing of others:
Holy Spirit, we rejoice in your life-giving power,
and ask that you will use the skills of doctors,
nurses and all who serve the sick. Give them love
and compassion, that they may be your ministers of
healing.

Lord God, we bring to you these our prayers, and ask
you to use them to further your gracious purpose for
your world: in the name of Jesus Christ, the healer of
all our sicknesses. **Amen.**

14 The Lord's Prayer

15 The Laying on of Hands

Invite those wishing this ministry to come forward.

16 Prayer for Healing

Lord Jesus, the same yesterday, today and for ever,
let your healing power be upon those who seek your
help at this time. Grant them new life and strength.

Each person should then come forward to kneel if possible.

(N...) may the Lord Christ grant you healing and
renewal, according to his will. Go in peace.

The person returns to his place.

17 Prayer of Thanksgiving

Father, we thank you that you have granted to each of

us a spiritual blessing, and that you are granting healing to your servants. Help us, refreshed by your presence, to go into the world, to serve you in the power of the Holy Spirit, through Jesus Christ our Lord. **Amen.**

18 Hymn

19 Dismissal and Blessing

A selection of Hymns and Bible Readings suitable for a Service for Healing.

Hymns

The Character of God
RCH—9, 17, 20, 22, 30, 232, 472.
CP —17, 37, 45, 57, 690.
CH3 —9, 25, 26, 35, 40, 151, 367.
NCP—4, 15, 29, 52, 57.

The Ministry and Person of Jesus Christ
RCH—86, 166, 191, 194, 277, 351.
CP —180, 204, 216, 469, 632, 668, 671, 672.
CH3 —52, 96, 103, 115, 214, 371, 525, 526.
NCP—14, 30, 31, 44.
SS —32.
HS —39.

The Christian Life
RCH—419, 439, 474, 487, 547, 559, 563.
CP —182, 398, 507, 549.
CH3 —90, 376, 461, 664, 669, 675.
NCP—26, 45, 73.
HT —73, 75.

RCH—Revised Church Hymnary.
NCP—New Church Praise.
HT —100 Hymns for Today.

CH3 —Church Hymnary Third Edition.
CP —Congregational Praise.
SS —Songs for the Seventies.
HS —Hymns and Songs.

Psalms

23, 27, 30, 34, 43, 46, 51, 86, 91, 103, 116, 121, 139, 143 (omit v 12).

Bible Readings

Isaiah 40: 1–11; 53: 4–12; 54: 7–10; 58: vv 1, 6, 9.
Matthew 5: 1–12; 6: 25–34.
Mark 1: 21–34; 2: 1–12; 9: 14–29.
Luke 7:18–23; 9: 1–6; 10: 1–9, 38–42; 11: 5–13.
John 9; 14: 12–17.
Acts 3: 1–16; 28: 7–10.
2 Corinthians 12: 7–10.
James 5: 13–16.

Service for the Laying of a Foundation Stone for a Church Building

1 Call to Worship

President:

Unless the Lord builds the house,
Its builders will have toiled in vain.
Unless the Lord keeps watch over a city,
in vain the watchman stands on guard.

The Lord says

See how I lay in Zion a stone of witness, a precious cornerstone, a foundation stone: the believer shall not stumble. And I will make justice the measure, integrity the plumb-line

By your grace, O Lord, go before us in everything that we do, and support us with your continuing help: so that in all our actions—begun, continued and ended in you—we may glorify your holy name, and finally by your mercy obtain everlasting life: through Jesus Christ our Lord. **Amen.**

2 Reading(s)

The following are appropriate:

Old Testament
Genesis 28: 10–22; Psalm 27: 1–5, 13–14; Isaiah 44: 24–28.

New Testament
1 Corinthians 3: 5–11; 1 Peter 1: 25–2:10; Revelation
        21: 1–6.

3 Stone Laying

President:

We have met together to lay the foundation stone of
our new church, and to dedicate it to the work and to
the glory of God.

In doing so we make this stone a symbol of our belief
in God's promises to us and of our confidence for the
future, and by using this symbol we are asking God's
blessing on our new enterprise and rededicating
ourselves to his service.

Here whoever is to lay the stone does so, and says:

We set this stone to stand here as a sign and as a
memorial: in the name of the Father and of the Son
and of the Holy Spirit.   **Amen.**

4 Prayer

President:

Lord God, by the leading of the Holy Spirit we have
come to this moment when we found a new church
building: our minds overflow now with thankfulness
for that leading, with joy in having made the first part
of our journey, and with trust that you will guide us
in the time to come.

We ask your blessing on the stone that we have set
here: may it for many generations be a witness to our
confidence in your power, and to our love for you and
our fellow-men.

People:

The word of the Lord stands fast for ever.

President

We ask your blessing on the building that is to stand here; may it be a landmark and a light to many, and a place where many learn your truth. May it praise you by its strength and permanence, and reflect your glory by its craftmanship and design.

People:

The word of the Lord stands fast for ever.

President:

We pray for all those who will labour to create a place of worship here: for architect, builders and decorators; and for all those who will share in the undertaking by their gifts of money and by their interest and help. May they have the happiness of seeing their work bear fruit and their aspirations become reality.

People:

The word of the Lord stands fast for ever.

President:

We pray for all those who will use this church: for adults and children who will worship here, and celebrate the sacraments; for those who in time to come will be baptized and married here and those who will be honoured here at their death.

We pray for those who will be leaders here, in preaching and teaching, in making music, in pastoral care and administration, and in fostering community. We pray for all who will clean and care for this building, decorate it with flowers, and offer their gifts; and for all who will love it and feel at home in it, both in our own generation and generations to come.

People:

The word of the Lord stands fast for ever.

President:

We pray for ourselves and for the part each of us has to play in making this new church a place where your presence may be known.

Remembering all your goodness to us in the past, and your faithfulness, we dedicate ourselves again to serve you both in word and action, and to live out our faith, in your church and in the world.

People:

The word of the Lord stands fast for ever.

All:

May the grace of our Lord Jesus Christ, and the love of God, and the fellowship of the Holy Spirit, be with us all.   Amen.

5 Hymn or Doxology

6 Dismissal and Blessing

A short list of hymns appropriate to the above service:

Congregational Praise—42, 237, 254, 261, 322, 340, 461, 520, 557, 657, 753, 754.

Church Hymnary, Third Edition—10, 102, 303, 312, 368, 402, 420, 451, 469, 472, 487, 509, 593, 609, 668.

Service for the Dedication of a Church

If circumstances allow, the congregation may remain outside until the call to worship has been given and then follow the President and other leaders into the church.

The President (who is the Provincial Moderator or his deputy), the minister and those with them (who should include representatives of the Provincial Synod and the District Council) enter the church by the main door. The congregation stands.

1 **Call to worship** (*given while the ministerial party is at the door*).

President

Worship the Lord in gladness;
enter his presence with songs of
exultation.

Minister

Enter his gates with thanksgiving and his
courts with praise. Give thanks to him
and bless his name:

People

**For the Lord is good and his love is
everlasting, his constancy endures to all
generations.**

Or

President

> Lift up your heads, you gates,
> lift yourselves up, you everlasting doors,
> that the king of glory may come in.

People

> **Who is the king of glory?**

Minister

> The king of glory is the Lord of Hosts.

The ministerial party proceeds in silence to the communion table. Its members carry with them an open Bible, bread and wine, and water for the font (with other appropriate symbols if desired), and place these on the communion table. The President remains at the communion table; the other members of the party now take their places for the service.

2 Hymn

3 Prayer *(minister):*

> God our Father, you are the Lord of all creation, and your purpose of love embraces us all and all that you have made.
>
> Help us to love you in return with all our heart and with all our soul and with all our strength.
>
> We are glad to share in your purpose to bring peace and reconciliation into the world through your Son Jesus Christ.
>
> We confess even as we respond to you, that our love is incomplete and we cannot show your glory to the world as your children should.
>
> We confess the hindrances we still put in your way as people and as churches; and we confess that our world

is spoiled by evil and unhappiness, and that Christ does not have his rightful place as Lord of life.

Forgive us, then, for what we have been and for what we still are.

May your Holy Spirit take hold of our lives and the life of this church, transforming what is wrong and giving us power to be your true servants, your friends, your children: through Jesus Christ our Lord. **Amen.**

4 Reading(s)

The following are appropriate:

Old Testament

Genesis 28: 10–22; 1 Kings 8: 22–30; Psalm 27: 1–10, 13–14; Psalm 84: 1–7, 10–12.

New Testament

John 10: 1–18; John 15: 1–17; Ephesians 1: 3–23; Philippians 2: 1–11; Colossians 3: 1–4, 12–17; 1 John 4: 7–21.

5 Hymn

6 Dedication

The President, at the communion table, says:

We have met together to praise God, to thank him for his gifts to us and for his leading of us, and to dedicate this church to his work and to his glory. Let us stand to join in the prayer of dedication.

President:

God our Father, we believe that your church is your people, and that it is called to bring to the world knowledge of your greatness, your mercy and your love.

We praise and thank you for the beauty of your creation; for the richness and variety of the world in which we are set; for the lives and minds of other people; and for the truths you show to us in worship, in the reading and preaching of your Word, and in the church's celebration of the sacraments.

Especially we thank you now for the human gifts which have gone into the making of this church: for the vision to plan; the skill to design; the ability to build; and the generosity to provide.

People:

> **By coming and offering ourselves in faith we show that this building is your house.**
>
> **Father, you are with us here. May your light and love always be known, in us and in this place.**

President:

Lord Jesus, we believe that the church is your Body in the world, and that as you have shown us the Father the church must show you to the world.

We praise and thank you that you are among us as our example of love and selflessness, and as our Saviour and our Lord. We believe that we meet you when we come together to share in prayer and in sacrament.

People:

> **By bringing in bread and wine and water we show that this building is your house.**
>
> **Lord Jesus, you are with us here. May your grace and truth always be known, in us and in this place.**

President:

Holy Spirit, we believe that it was by your inspiration

and your power that we were all led to join together
our individual lives in a Christian congregation, and
to build (or set aside) this house as a meeting place
with each other and with you.

We praise and thank you that you come to us as our
helper, our joy in times of delight and insight and our
comfort in times of hopelessness and grief. We believe
that you will be the light to guide us through the
changing days of the future.

People:

**By bringing in the Bible, we show that this
building is your house.**

**Holy Spirit, you are with us here. May your
guidance and strength always be known, in us
and in this place.**

President:

Father, Son and Holy Spirit, we dedicate this church
building to your work and to your glory. We pray for
your continued presence, so that the faith of those
who worship here may be made stronger, their hope
made brighter, and their love made deeper.

May this church be a place where many come to you
and learn to know you. May your gospel be both
preached and demonstrated here.

Together with this building, we dedicate again our
lives and our gifts to you. Give us grace to serve:
doing and bearing your will, sharing always and in
every way in the Church's work, giving and receiving
love.

We remember that your church here is one small
branch of your great and historic family. We pray that
by the new life and new energy made evident here we
may play our part in your whole Church's task,
drawing all the world towards your love.

People:

**Lord, we are your people. Give us insight and
courage to do your work, in this church and
wherever we may be.**

President:

We join with all your people in the Lord's Prayer:
Our Father...

7 Hymn

8 An Address *may be given here*

9 Intercessions

*These may appropriately include prayers for the future life
of the church, its witness and the place it will play in the
wider community; for those who will use it—for marriage,
baptisms, funerals, for worship and for recreational
purposes; and for the wider Church.*

10 Offering

*At this point a celebration of the Lord's Supper may
follow.*

11 Hymn

12 Dismissal and Blessing

A short list of hymns appropriate to the above service.

Congregational Praise—210, 224, 237, 238, 246, 248,
        258, 259, 265, 269, 520, 657, 660, 730.

New Church Praise—10, 29, 102.

Church Hymnary, Third Edition—10, 13, 15, 94, 102,
        107, 117, 119, 334, 355, 390, 509, 566(ii), 610.

> We praise your name O God of all creation
> (Fred Kaan, *Pilgrim Praise*)

Prayers for the Dedication of Church Property

The Minister, together with any assisting him, goes to the part of the church where the act of dedication is to take place. This could appropriately be after the offerings have been received, though the nature of the property to be dedicated will decide the timing of the dedication (an organ, for example, might be dedicated at the beginning of a service).

Minister:

Unless the Lord builds the house,
its builders will have toiled in vain.
Unless the Lord keeps watch over a city,
in vain the watchman stands on guard.

By your grace, O Lord, go before us in everything that we do, and support us with your continuing help: so that in all our actions—begun, continued and ended in you—we may glorify your holy name, and finally by your mercy obtain everlasting life: through Jesus Christ our Lord. **Amen.**

We are now to dedicate this ... to the glory of God (and in memory of our friend AB.)

Prayers of dedication

For a font or baptistery

God our Father, the whole of our world is your creation, and in bringing gifts to you we bring only what is yours. We now dedicate to you this font/baptistery, praising you for the inspiration which led to its designing, for the skill of mind and eye that planned it, and for the craftmanship that made it.

We set it apart now to serve the work of your church in the celebration of the sacrament of baptism.

May it add to the beauty and joy of worship here, and give inspiration and happiness to generations of your people: and may your name be glorified through it. **Amen.**

For a Bible:

God our Father, the whole of our world is your creation, and in bringing gifts to you we bring only what is yours. We now dedicate to you this Bible, praising you for the depth and richness of your Word and for the skills of translator, printer and binder that have brought it to us here.

We offer it now to you, to serve the work of your church in bringing the recreating news of your love and your forgiveness to all who read and all who listen.

May it add to the beauty and joy of worship here, and give inspiration and happiness to generations of your people: and may your name be glorified through it. **Amen.**

For a lectern or a pulpit:

God our Father, the whole of our world is your creation, and in bringing gifts to you we bring only what is yours. We now dedicate to you this lectern/pulpit, praising you for the inspiration which led to its designing, for the skill of the mind and eye that planned it, and for the craftmanship that made it.

We set it apart now to serve the work of your church in bringing the recreating news of your love and your forgiveness to all who are in this place.

F

May it add to the beauty and joy of worship here, and give inspiration and happiness to generations of your people; and may your name be glorified through it. **Amen.**

For an Organ:

God our Father, the whole of our world is your creation, and in bringing gifts to you we bring only what is yours. We now dedicate to you this Organ, praising you for the inspiration which led to its designing, for the skill of the mind and eye that planned it, and for the craftmanship that made it.

We set it apart now to serve the work of your church in the ministry of music, both when we sing and when we listen.

May it add to the beauty and joy of worship here, and give inspiration and happiness to generations of your people; and may your name be glorified through it. **Amen.**

For a communion table or vessels:

God our Father, the whole of our world is your creation, and in bringing gifts to you we bring only what is yours. We now dedicate to you this table/these vessels, praising you for the inspiration which led to its/their designing, for the skill of the mind and eye that planned it/them, and for the craftmanship that made it/them.

We set it/them apart now to serve the work of your church in uniting your people in love and adoration when they eat your supper together at your table.

May it/they add to the beauty and joy of worship here, and give inspiration and happiness to generations of your people: and may your name be glorified through it/them. **Amen.**

When the property to be dedicated is the gift of someone still living, this prayer may follow:

The giving of gifts binds us to each other and unites us to you, Giver of all. We remember before you now our friend AB, thanking you for the generosity of his/her mind. May this . . . . be a reminder to us of the communion of saints, and, whenever we remember, may we be thankful. Through Jesus Christ our Lord. **Amen.**

When the property to be dedicated is given in memory of someone now dead, this prayer may follow:

Eternal God, we remember before you now our friend AB, thanking you for his/her life. As long as we live, may this . . . . be a reminder to us of the communion of saints, and whenever we remember, may we be thankful. Through Jesus Christ our Lord. **Amen.**

The act of dedication may close with a Doxology.

Creeds and Canticles

Apostles' Creed

I believe in God, the Father almighty,
  creator of heaven and earth.

I believe in Jesus Christ, his only Son, our Lord.
  He was conceived by the power of the Holy Spirit
    and born of the Virgin Mary.
  He suffered under Pontius Pilate, was crucified,
    died, and was buried.
  He descended to the dead.
  On the third day he rose again.
  He ascended into heaven
    and is seated at the right hand of the Father.
  He will come again to judge the living and the
    dead.

I believe in the Holy Spirit,
  the holy catholic Church,
  the communion of saints,
  the forgiveness of sins,
  the resurrection of the body,
  and the life everlasting.   Amen.

Nicene Creed

We believe in one God,
   the Father, the Almighty,
   maker of heaven and earth,
   of all that is, seen and unseen.

We believe in one Lord, Jesus Christ,
   the only Son of God,
   eternally begotten of the Father,
   God from God, Light from Light,
   true God from true God,
   begotten, not made,
   of one Being with the Father.
   Through him all things were made.
   For us men and for our salvation he came down
      from heaven:
   by the power of the Holy Spirit he became
      incarnate from the Virgin Mary, and was made
      man.
   For our sake he was crucified under Pontius Pilate;
      he suffered death and was buried.
      On the third day he rose again in accordance with
         the Scriptures;
      he ascended into heaven and is seated at the right
         hand of the Father.
   He will come again in glory to judge the living and
      the dead, and his kingdom will have no end.

We believe in the Holy Spirit, the Lord, the giver of
      life,
   who proceeds from the Father [and the Son].
   With the Father and the Son he is worshipped and
      glorified.
   He has spoken through the Prophets.
   We believe one holy catholic and apostolic
      Church.
   We acknowledge one baptism for the forgiveness of
      sins.
   We look for the resurrection of the dead, and the
      life of the world to come.   Amen.

The Confession of Faith of The United Reformed Church

We believe in one living and true God,
creator, preserver and ruler of all things in heaven and
    earth,
Father, Son and holy Spirit:

> Him alone we worship, and in him we put our
>   trust.

We believe that God, in his infinite love for men,
gave his eternal Son, Jesus Christ our Lord,
who became man,
lived on earth in perfect love and obedience,
died upon the cross for our sins,
rose again from the dead:

> And lives for evermore, saviour, judge and king.

We believe that, by the Holy Spirit,
this glorious gospel is made effective
so that through faith we receive the forgiveness of
        sins,
newness of life as children of God
and strength in this present world to do his will.
We believe in one, holy, catholic, apostolic Church,
in heaven and on earth,
wherein by the same Spirit,
the whole company of believers is made one Body of
        Christ:

> To worship God and serve him and all men, in his
>   kingdom of righteousness and love.

We rejoice in the gift of eternal life,
        and believe that, in the fulness of time,
God will renew and gather in one all things in
        Christ,
to whom with the Father and the Holy Spirit,
be glory and majesty, dominion and power,
both now and ever.   Amen.

This confession may be made responsively, with the people saying the lines indented. Leader and people may say the last six lines together.

———————

Te Deum

You are God: we praise you;
You are the Lord: we acclaim you;
You are the eternal Father:
All creation worships you.
To you all angels, all the powers of heaven,
Cherubim and Seraphim, sing in endless praise:
    Holy, holy, holy Lord, God of power and might,
    heaven and earth are full of your glory.
The glorious company of apostles praise you.
The noble fellowship of prophets praise you.
The white-robed army of martyrs praise you.
Throughout the world the holy Church acclaims you:
    Father, of majesty unbounded,
    your true and only Son, worthy of all worship,
    and the Holy Spirit, advocate and guide.
You, Christ, are the king of glory,
the eternal Son of the Father.
When you became man to set us free
you did not abhor the Virgin's womb.
You overcame the sting of death,
and opened the kingdom of heaven to all believers.
You are seated at God's right hand in glory.
We believe that you will come, and be our judge.
    Come then, Lord, and help your people,
    bought with the price of your own blood,
    and bring us with your saints
    to glory everlasting.

Responses after the *Te Deum*

Save your people, Lord, and bless your
    inheritance.
Govern and uphold them now and always.
Day by day we bless you.
We praise your name for ever.
Keep us today, Lord, from all sin.
Have mercy on us, Lord, have mercy.
Lord, show us your love and mercy;
for we put our trust in you.
In you, Lord, is our hope:
and we shall never hope in vain.

Benedictus

Blessed be the Lord, the God of Israel;
he has come to his people and set them free.
He has raised up for us a mighty saviour.
born of the house of his servant David.
Through his holy prophets he promised of old
    that he would save us from our enemies,
    from the hands of all who hate us.
He promised to show mercy to our fathers and to
       remember his holy covenant.
This was the oath he swore to our father Abraham:
to set us free from the hands of our enemies,
free to worship him without fear,
holy and righteous in his sight
    all the days of our life

You, my child, shall be called the prophet of the
       Most High,
for you will go before the Lord to prepare his way.
to give his people knowledge of salvation by the
       forgiveness of all their sins.
In the tender compassion of our God
the dawn from on high shall break upon us,
to shine on those who dwell in darkness and the
       shadow of death,
and to guide our feet into the way of peace.

F*

Magnificat

My soul proclaims the greatness of the Lord,
my spirit rejoices in God my Saviour;
for he has looked in favour on his lowly servant.
From this day all generations will call me blessed:
the Almighty has done great things for me,
and holy is his Name.
He has mercy on those who fear him
in every generation
He has shown the strength of his arm,
he has scattered the proud in their conceit.
He has cast down the mighty from their thrones,
and has lifted up the lowly.
He has filled the hungry with good things,
and the rich he has sent away empty.
He has come to the help of his servant Israel
for he has remembered his promise of mercy,
the promise he made to our fathers,
to Abraham and his children for ever.

Nunc Dimittis

Lord, now you let your servant go in peace;
   your word has been fulfilled:
my own eyes have seen the salvation
   which you have prepared in the sight of every
      people:
a light to reveal you to the nations
   and the glory of your people Israel.

Agnus Dei

Jesus, Lamb of God:
   have mercy on us.
Jesus, bearer of our sins:
   have mercy on us.
Jesus, redeemer of the world:
   give us your peace.

Gloria Patri

Glory to the Father, and to the Son,
   and to the Holy Spirit:
as it was in the beginning, is now,
   and shall be for ever.   Amen.

Calendar and Lectionary

1. These lessons are based on the proposals of the Joint Liturgical Group. Three lessons are given for the main Sunday Service. The 'controlling' lection is printed in **bold type.** If only one lesson is used it is desirable that it should be this one.

2. The Lectionary is planned so that the first year cycle is begun to be read on the 9th Sunday before Christmas in years with an even number (1980, 1982 . . .) and the second year cycle in years with an odd number (1981, 1983 . . .).

3. The theme titles illustrate an aspect of the lessons but should be understood as guides only and not as limitations to the use of the scriptures. Where two themes are given the first relates to the lessons of the first year and the second to those of the second year.

Sunday	Year 1	Year 2	Theme
9 before Christmas	**Gen. 1. 1–3, 24–31a**	**Gen. 2. 4b–9, 15–25**	The Creation
	Col. 1.15–20	Rev. 4	
	John 1. 1–14	John 3. 1–8	
8 before Christmas	**Gen. 4.1–10**	**Gen. 3.1–15**	The Fall
	1 John 3.9–18	Rom. 7.7–13	
	Mark 7. 14–23	John 3. 13–21	
7 before Christmas	**Gen. 12.1–9**	**Gen. 22.1–18**	The Election of God's
	Rom. 4. 13–25	Jas. 2. 14–24 (25, 26)	People: Abraham
	John 8. 51–58	Luke 20. 9–17	

6 before Christmas	Exod. 3. 7-15 Heb. 3. 1-6 John 6. 25-35	Exod. 6. 2-8 Heb. 11. 17-31 Mark 13. 5-13	The Promise of Redemption: Moses
5 before Christmas	1 Kings 19. 9-18 Rom. 11. 13-24 Matt. 24. 37-44	Isa. 10. 20-23 Rom. 9. 19-28 Mark 13. 14-23	The Remnant of Israel
4 before Christmas (Advent 1)	Isa. 52. 7-10 1 Thess. 5. 1-11 Luke 21. 25-33	Isa. 51. 4-11 Rom. 13. 8-14 Matt. 25. 31-46	The Advent Hope
3 before Christmas (Advent 2)	Isa. 55. 1-11 2 Tim. 3. 14-4. 5 John 5. 36b-47	Isa. 64. 1-7 Rom. 15. 4-13 Luke 4. 14-21	The Word of God in the Old Testament
2 before Christmas (Advent 3)	Isa. 40. 1-11 1 Cor. 4. 1-5 John 1. 19-28	Mal. 3. 1-5 Phil. 4. 4-9 Matt. 11. 2-15	The Forerunner
1 before Christmas (Advent 4)	Isa. 11. 1-9 1. Cor. 1. 26-31 Luke 1. 26-38a	Zech. 2. 10-13 Rev. 21. 1-7 Matt. 1. 18-23	The Annunciation
Christmas Eve and Chstismas Day	Isa. 9. 2. 6-7 or Isa. 62. 10-12 or Micah. 5. 2-4 Titus 2. 11-14; 3. 3-7 or 1 John 4. 7-14 or Heb. 1. 1-15 (6-12) **Luke 2. 1-14 (15-20)** or **Luke 2. 8-20** or **John 1. 1-14**		The Birth of Jesus

Sunday	Year 1	Year 2	Theme
Christmas 1	Isa. 7. 10–14 Gal. 4. 1–7 **John 1. 14–18**	1 Sam. 1. 20–28 Rom. 12. 1–8 **Luke 2. 21–40**	The Incarnation The Presentation in the Temple
Christmas 2	Ecclus. 3. 2–7 or Exod. 12. 21–27 Rom. 8. 11–17 **Luke 2. 41–52**	Isa. 60. 1–6 Rev. 21.22–22.5 **Matt. 2. 1–12, 19–23**	The Holy Family/ The Wise Men
If Epiphany is celebrated on 6th January the lessons may be Isa. 49. 1–6, Eph. 3. 1–12, **Matt. 2. 1–12.**			
Christmas 3	1 Sam. 16. 1–13a Acts. 10. 34–38a **Matt. 3. 13–17**	Isa. 42. 1–7 Eph. 2. 1–10 **John 1. 29–34**	Revelation: The Baptism of Jesus
Christmas 4	Jer. 1. 4–10 Acts 26. 1, 9–20 **Mark 1. 14–20**	1 Sam. 3. 1–10 Gal. 1. 11–24 **John 1. 35–51**	Revelation: The First Disciples
Christmas 5	Exod. 33. 12–23 1 John 1. 1–7 **John 2. 1–11**	Deut. 8. 1–6 Phil. 4. 10–20 **John 6. 1–14**	Revelation: Signs of Glory
Christmas 6	1 Kings 8. 22–30 1 Cor. 3. 10–17 **John 2. 13–22**	Jer. 7. 1–11 Heb. 12. 18–29 **John 4. 19–26**	Revelation: The New Temple

Christmas 7	Prov. 2. 1–9 or Ecclus. 42. 15–25 1 Cor. 3. 18–23 Matt. 12. 38–42	2 Sam. 12. 1–10 Rom. 1. 18–25 Matt. 13. 24–30	Revelation: The Wisdom of God/ Parables
Christmas 8	Isa. 1. 10–17 (Years 1 and 2) 1 Cor. 3. 18–23 Mark 2. 23–3. 6		The Sabbath
9 before Easter	Isa. 30. 18–21 1 Cor. 4. 8–13 Matt. 5. 1–12	Prov. 3. 1–8 1 Cor. 2. 1–10 Luke 8. 4–15	Christ the Teacher
8 before Easter	Zeph. 3. 14–20 Jas. 5. 13–16a Mark 2. 1–12	2 Kings 5. 1–14 2 Cor. 12. 1–10 Mark 7. 24–37	Christ the Healer
7 before Easter	Hosea 14. 1–7 Philemon 1–16 Mark 2. 13–17	Num. 15. 32–36 Col. 1. 18–23 John 8. 2–11	Christ the Friend of Sinners
Ash Wednesday	Isa. 58. 1–8 or Joel 2. 12–17 1 Cor. 9. 24–27 Matt. 6. 16–21 or [Amos 5. 6–15 Jas. 4. 1–10 Luke 18. 9–14]		

Sunday	Year 1	Year 2	Theme
6 before Easter (Lent 1)	Gen. 2. 7–9; 3. 1–7 Heb. 2. 14–18 **Matt. 4. 1–11**	Gen. 4. 1–10 Heb. 4. 12–16 **Luke 4. 1–13**	The King and the Kingdom: Temptation
5 before Easter (Lent 2)	Gen. 6. 11–22 1 John 4. 1–6 **Luke 19. 41–48**	Gen. 7. 17–24 1 John 3. 1–10 **Matt. 12. 22–32**	The King and the Kingdom: Conflict
4 before Easter (Lent 3)	Gen. 22. 1–13 Col. 1. 24–29 **Luke 9. 18–27**	Gen. 12. 1–9 1 Pet. 2. 19–25 **Matt. 16. 13–28**	The King and the Kingdom: Suffering
3 before Easter (Lent 4)	Exod. 34. 29–35 2 Cor. 3. 4–18 **Luke 9. 28–36**	Exod. 3. 1–6 2 Pet. 1. 16–19 **Matt. 17. 1–13**	The King and the Kingdom: Transfiguration
2 before Easter (Passion Sunday)	Exod. 6. 2–13 Col. 2. 8–15 **John 12. 20–32**	Jer. 31. 31–34 Heb. 9. 11–14 **Mark 10. 32–45**	The King and the Kingdom: The Victory of the Cross
1 before Easter (Palm Sunday)	Isa. 50. 4–9a ⎤ Phil. 2. 5–11 ⎟ or **Mark 14. 32–15. 4** ⎦	⎡ Zech. 9. 9–12 ⎟ 1 Cor. 1. 18–25 ⎣ **Matt. 21. 1–13**	The Way of the Cross
Maundy Thursday	Exod. 12. 1–14 1 Cor. 11. 23–29 **John 13. 1–15**	Jer. 31. 31–34 1 Cor. 10. 16–17 **Mark 14. 12–26**	The Institution of the Eucharist and The New Commandment

Good Friday	Isa. 52. 13–53. 12 Heb. 10. 11–25 or **John 18. 1–19. 37** or	Heb. 4. 14-16; 5. 7–9 **John 19. 1–37**	The Cross
			The Resurrection
Easter Day	Gen 1. 1–15, 26–28, 31 Exod. 4. 27–5. 1 Exod. 14. 21–31 Rom. 6. 3–11 **Matt. 28. 1–10**	⌈ Isa. 12 or Isa. 43. 16-21 Rev. 1. 10–18 or or 1 Cor. 15. 12–20 or Col. 3. 1–11 **John 20. 1–10 (or 18)** or ⌊ **Mark 16. 1–8**	
Easter 1	Exod. 15. 1–11 1 Pet. 1. 3–9 **John 20. 19–29**	Exod. 16. 2–15 1 Cor. 15. 53–58 **John 6. 32–40**	The Upper Room/ The Bread of Life
Easter 2	Exod. 25. 6–9 Rev. 19. 6–9 **Luke 24. 13–35**	Ezek. 34. 7–16 1 Pet. 5. 1–11 **John 10. 7–16**	The Emmaus Road/ The Good Shepherd
Easter 3	Isa. 61. 1–7 1 Cor. 15. 1–11 **John 21. 1–14**	1 Kings 17. 17-24 Col. 3. 1–11 **John 11. 17–27**	The Lakeside/ The Resurrection and the Life
Easter 4	Isa. 62. 1–5 Rev. 3. 14–22 **John 21. 15–22**	Prov. 4. 10–19 2 Cor. 4. 13–5. 5 **John 14. 1–11**	The Charge to Peter/ The Way, the Truth, and the Life
Easter 5	Hosea 6. 1–6 1 Cor. 15. 21–28 **John 16. 25–33**	Deut. 34 Rom. 8. 28–39 **John 16. 12–24**	Going to the Father

Sunday	Year 1	Year 2	Theme
Ascension Day	Dan. 7. 9–14 Acts 1. 1–11 (Years 1 and 2) **Matt. 28.16–20**		The Ascension of Christ
Easter 6	Dan. 7. 9–14 Eph. 1. 15–23 **Luke 24. 45–53**	2 Kings 2. 1–15 Eph. 4.1–13 **Luke 24. 45–53**	The Ascension of Christ
Pentecost	Gen. 11. 1–9 **Acts 2.1–11** John 14. 15–26 ⎤ ⎥ or ⎦	Exod.19.16–25 **Acts 2. 1–11** John 20. 19–23	The Gift of the Spirit
Pentecost 1 (Trinity)	Isa. 6.1–8 **Eph. 1. 3–14** John 14. 8–17	Deut. 6. 4–9 **Acts 2. 22–24 (25–31) 32–36** Matt. 11. 25–30	The Unity and Riches of God
Pentecost 2	Exod. 19. 1–6 **1 Pet. 2.1–10** John 15. 1–5	2 Sam. 7. 4–16 **Acts 2. 37–47** Luke 14. 15–24	The People of God/ The Church's Unity and Fellowship
Pentecost 3	Deut. 6. 17–25 **Rom. 6. 3–11** John 15. 5–11	Deut. 8. 11–20 **Acts 4. 8–12** Luke 8. 41–55	The Life of the Baptised/ The Church's Confidence in Christ
Pentecost 4	Deut. 7.6–11 **Gal. 3.23–4.7** John 15.12–17	Isa. 63. 7–14 **Acts 8. 26–38** Luke 15. 1–10	The Freedom of the Sons of God/The Church's Mission to the Individual

Pentecost 5	Exod. 20. 1–17 **Eph. 5. 1–10** Matt. 19. 16–26	Ruth 1. 8–17, 22 **Acts 11. 4–18** Luke 10. 1–12	The Church's Mission to All Mankind The New Law
Pentecost 6	Exod. 24. 3–11 **Col. 3. 12–17** Luke 15. 11–32	Micah. 6. 1–8 **Eph. 4. 17–32** Mark 10. 46–52	The New Humanity
Pentecost 7	Hosea 11. 1–9 **1 Cor. 12. 27–13. 13** Matt. 18. 21–35	Deut. 10. 12–11. 1 **Rom. 8. 1–11** Mark 12. 28–34	The More Excellent Way
Pentecost 8	Ezek. 36. 24–28 **Gal. 5. 16–25** John 15. 16–27	Ezek. 37. 1–14 **1 Cor. 12. 4–13** Luke 6. 27–38	The Fruit of The Spirit
Pentecost 9	Josh. 1. 1–9 **Eph. 6. 10–20** John 17. 11b–19	1 Sam. 17. 37–50 **2 Cor. 6. 3–10** Mark 9. 14–29	The Whole Armour of God
Pentecost 10	Job. 42. 1–6 **Phil. 2. 1–11** John 13. 1–15	1 Sam. 24. 9–17 or 1–17 **Gal. 6. 1–10** Luke 7. 36–50	The Mind of Christ
Pentecost 11	Isa. 42. 1–7 **2 Cor. 4. 1–10** John 13. 31–35	1 Chron. 29. 1–9 **Phil. 1. 1–11** Matt. 20. 1–16	The Serving Community

Sunday	Year 1	Year 2	Theme
Pentecost 12	Isa. 49. 1–6 **2 Cor. 5.14–6. 2** John 17. 20–26	Micah 4. 1–5 **Acts 17. 22–31** Matt. 5. 13–16	The Witnessing Community
Pentecost 13	Isa. 50. 4–9a **Acts 7. 54–8. 1** John 16. 1–11	Jer. 20.7–11a **Acts 20. 17–35** Matt. 10. 16–22	The Suffering Community
Pentecost 14	Prov. 31.10–31 **Eph. 5. 25–6.4** Mark 10. 2–16	Gen. 45.1–15 **Eph. 3.14–21** Luke 11. 1–13	The Family
Pentecost 15	Isa. 45. 1–7 **Rom. 13. 1–7** Matt. 22. 15–22	1 Kings 3. 4–15 **1 Tim. 2. 1–7** Matt. 14. 1–2	Those in Authority
Pentecost 16	Lev. 19. 9–18 **Rom. 12. 9–21** Luke 10. 25–37	Deut. 15. 7–11 **1 John 4. 15–21** Luke 16. 19–31	The Neighbour
Pentecost 17	Jer. 7. 1–7 **James 1. 16–27** Luke 17. 11–19	Jer. 32. 6–15 **Gal. 2. 15–3. 9** Luke 7. 1–10	The Proof of Faith
Pentecost 18	Deut. 26. 1–11 **2 Cor. 8. 1–9** Matt. 5. 17–26	Nehemiah 6. 1–16 or Ecclus. 38. 24–34 **1 Pet. 4. 7–11** Matt. 25. 14–30	The Offering of Life

Pentecost 19	Gen. 28. 10–22 **Heb. 11. 1–2, 8–16** Matt. 6. 24–34	Dan. 6. 10–23 **Rom. 5. 1–11** Luke 19. 1–10	The Life of Faith
Pentecost 20	Dan. 3. 13–26 **Rom. 8. 18–25** Luke 9. 51–62	Gen. 32. 22–30 **1 Cor. 9. 19–27** Matt. 7. 13–27	Endurance
Pentecost 21	Hab. 2. 1–4 **Acts 26. 1–8** Luke 18. 1–8	Ezek. 12. 21–28 **1 Pet. 1. 13–21** John 11. 17–27	The Christian Hope
Pentecost 22	Deut. 11. 18–28 (Years 1 and 2) **1 John 2. 22–29** Luke 16. 1–9		The Two Ways
Last Sunday after Pentecost	Jer. 29. 1, 4–14 **Phil. 3. 7–21** John 17. 1–10	Isa. 33. 17–22 **Rev. 7. 2–4, 9–17** Matt. 25. 1–13	Citizens of Heaven
Church Anniversary or Dedication Festival	2 Chron. 7. 11–16 or 1 Kings 8. 22–30 or Gen. 28. 10–22 Heb. 10. 19–25 or 1 Pet. 2. 1–5 or Rev. 21. 9–14, 22–27 John 10. 22–29 or Matt. 21. 12–16 or Matt. 12. 1–21		
Harvest	Gen. 8. 15–22 or Deut. 8. 1–10 or Deut. 26. 1–11 Rev. 14. 14–18 or Acts 14. 13–17 or 1 Tim. 6. 6–10 Mark 4. 1–9 or Luke 12. 16–31 or Matt. 13. 24–33		

Sunday

All Saints
Jer. 31. 31–34 or Isa. 66. 20–23
Heb. 11. 32–12. 2(18–24) or Rev. 7. 2–4, 9–12
Matt. 5. 1–11(12) or Luke 6. 20–23

Remembrance and Peace
Isa 52. 7–12 or Micah 4. 3–5 or 2 Sam. 23. 13–17
Rev. 22. 1–5 or 1 Tim. 2. 1–5 or Rom. 8. 31–35, 37–39
John 15. 9–17 or Matt. 5. 43–48 or Matt. 5. 1–12

Church Unity
Jer. 33. 6–9a or Deut. 6. 4–9 or Isa. 11. 1–9
Eph. 4. 1–6(16) or Eph. 2. 11–22 or 1 Corr. 3. 1–11
John 17. 11b–23 or John 17. 20–26 or John 15. 1–11

Education
Prov. 3. 13–17 or Job 28. 12–28
Acts 17. 16–34 or 1 Tim. 4. 9–16
Luke 2. 41–52 or Matt. 13. 44–58

Civic and Social Responsibility
Deut. 5. 1–21 or Amos 5. 21–24 or Isa. 58. 1–8
Phil. 2. 1–11 or Acts 5. 1–11 or Rom. 14. 1–9
Mark 10. 42–45 or Matt. 25. 31–41 or Matt. 5. 43–48

World Mission
Isa. 42. 1–9 or Isa. 49. 1–6 or Isa. 52. 7–10
Rom. 1. 8–17 or Acts 16. 1–10 or Rom. 10. 5–17
John 3. 1–16 or Matt. 28. 16–20 or Luke 10. 1–9

Psalms for use with the Lectionary

The following selection of psalms or portions of psalms suitable for use with the lectionary theme of a particular day are chosen because they appear in one or more of the hymn books used in the United Reformed Church, viz. Church Hymnary: Third Edition, Congregational Praise and New Church Praise. The psalm first referred to can appropriately be used to 'link' the Old and New Testament Lessons. Certain verses from the psalms or canticle suggested can be used as a call to worship at the beginning of the service. If a psalm has a particular character, eg. penitence, thanksgiving, it can be used at the appropriate point in worship for this.

Sunday	Psalms	Church Hymnary	Congregational Praise
9 before Christmas	104: 1-9. 8. *The Strain Upraise*	35.138.—	17, 849. 800. 796
8 before Christmas	130. 86	65, 66, 67. 321 *Also 77 in New Church Praise*	381, 382, 860. 383, 838
7 before Christmas	93. 1. 136	140. —. 137, 350, 33	737, 843. 797. 44, 861
6 before Christmas	77:11-20.	—.101	835. 740
5 before Christmas	106:1-14, 39-48 130. *Salvator Mundi*	381, 382, 860. 794	381, 382, 860. 794
4 before Christmas (Advent 1)	98. 50. 96	65, 66, 67.— *Also 77 in New Church Praise* 348, 349. 310. 22 *Also 66 and 89 in New Church Praise*	792. —. 844
3 before Christmas (Advent 2)	19:7-15. 119:33-40	125, 126, 143. 127	30, 318, 592, 804. —

Sunday	Psalms	Church Hymnary	Congregational Praise
2 before Christmas (Advent 3)	Benedictus 126	161. 393	784.—
1 before Christmas (Advent 4)	Magnificat 131	163, 164.— *Also 92 in New Church Praise*	785, 786. 441
Christmas Eve	2. 89:1-18	166. 390	—. 839
Christmas Day	85. 98	75, 321. 348, 349 *Also 66 and 89 in New Church Praise*	156, 837. 792
Christmas 1	8. 122	138. 489	800. 238, 607, 859
Christmas 2	72:1-19. *Nunc Dimittis*	158, 167, 413, 317. 204	158, 326, 834. 787
Christmas 3	36:5-10. 29	6.—	51, 817. 811
Christmas 4	145:1-12. 67	346. 493, 497, 598 *Also 65 in New Church Praise*	10, 743, 865. 330
Christmas 5	46. 119:1-16. *The Song of the Three*	24, 406, 407.—.—	485, 488, 733, 822. 857. 789
Christmas 6	84:1-7. 34. *The Song of the Three*	4. 391	257, 259, 735, 836. 46. 816, 790
Christmas 7	100. 138. 116:1-7	1, 2, 3, 17.—.—	1, 2, 788. 862. 855
Christmas 8	25:1-9. 43	74. 7 *Also refrain of 86 in New Church Praise*	809. 732, 821
9 before Easter	103:1-13. *Beatitudes*	351, 9.— *Also 86 in New Church Praise*	18, 45, 64, 739, 848. 793
8 before Easter	48. 46	—. 24, 406, 407	824. 485, 488, 733, 822
7 before Easter	139. 66	68.—	863. 832

Ash Wednesday	51:1-17.130	63,64.65,66,67	825.381,382,860 *Also 77 in New Church Praise*
6 before Easter (Lent 1)	51:1-17.91:1-12	63,64.—	825.841
5 before Easter (Lent 2)	18:1-24.119:33-40	—.127	59,803.—
4 before Easter (Lent 3)	42.115:1-8.55	231.—.—	390,821.854.826
3 before Easter (Lent 4)	84:1-13.36:5-10	4.6	257,259,735,836.51,51,817
2 before Easter (Passion Sunday)	22:22-28.143:1-11	239.70	806.864
1 before Easter (Palm Sunday)	24.22:1-19	566.239	730,808.806
Maundy Thursday	116:11-16.26:6-8	565.564	855.—
Good Friday	40.32.22:14-21. *The Reproaches*	73.—.239.240	731,820.814.806.—
Easter Day	118:14-29. *Easter Anthems. Te Deum*	262,263.—.345	604,856.783.781,782 *Also 21 in New Church Praise*
Easter 1	150.145:1-12	9,347,359.346	4,20,25,45,869,870. 10,743,865 *Also 65 and 80 in New Church Praise*
Easter 2	23.111	387,388,389.—	43,48,50,61,729,807.851

Sunday	Psalms	Church Hymnary	Congregational Praise
Easter 3	27. 16	26, 404. —	501, 810. 483, 802
Easter 4	33:1–12. 37:23–32	27. —	815. 818
Easter 5	65. 124	28. 392	7, 734, 831. —
Ascension Day	8. 24. 68	138. 566. 285	800. 146, 730, 808. —
Easter 6	47. 24	284. 566	823. 146, 730, 808.
Pentecost	98. 122. 104	348, 349. 389. 326	792. 238, 607, 742, 859. 849
		Also 66 and 89 in New Church Praise	
Pentecost 1 (Trinity)	97. Trisagion	—. 61, 240	845. —
Pentecost 2	95:1–7. 133	19, 20, 21. —	738, 779. 742
Pentecost 3	78. 102	547. 333	—. 847
Pentecost 4	63:1–9. 147:1–5	41. 136	403, 830. 57, 867
Pentecost 5	100. 96	1, 2, 3, 17. 22	1, 2, 788. 844
Pentecost 6	121. 112	139. —	741, 858. 852
Pentecost 7	62. 99	25. —	—. 846
Pentecost 8	25:1–9. 148	74. 135, 37	809. 4, 11, 13, 744, 868
		Also refrain of 86 in New Church Praise	
Pentecost 9	18:1–6, 30–36. 9	—. 23	59, 803. —
Pentecost 10	73:1–27. 4. 19	—. 125, 126, 143	592. 798. 30, 318, 592, 804
Pentecost 11	145:1–13. 31:1–6	346. —. —	10, 743, 865. 813
		Also 65 in New Church Praise	
Pentecost 12	150. 30	9, 347, 359. —	4, 20, 25, 45, 869, 870. 812
		Also 80 in New Church Praise	
Pentecost 13	43. 113	7. —	732, 821. 853
		Also 79 in New Church Praise	

Acknowledgements

A volume such as this naturally contains quotations, echoes and reflections from other publications in the same field. The Committee acknowledges its wide-ranging indebtedness, but trusts that there has been no infringement of copyright.

Thanks are due to the following for permission to use material as noted:

The Very Rev. R. C. D. Jasper, Dean of York, on behalf of the International Commission on English Texts for The Lord's Prayer (adapted) (p. 37): The Te Deum © 1970, '71, '75 (excerpts) (pp. 98 and 99); The Creeds and Canticles (p. 164).

The Very Rev. R. C. D. Jasper, Dean of York, on behalf of the Joint Liturgical Group for The Eucharistic Canon (p. 32), The Purpose of Marriage (adapted) (p. 69), and The Lectionary (adapted) (pp. 167–175) from *The Daily Office Revised* (S.P.C.K. 1978).

Collins Publishers for excerpts from *The Psalms: A New Translation for Worship*, © English Text 1976, 1977, David L. Frost, John A. Everton, Andrew A. Mackintosh, © pointing 1976, 1977 Wm. Collins Sons and Co. Ltd. (pp. 81–83).

Methodist Publishing House for The Promise (p. 77), and Prayer of Approach (p. 81) from *The Methodist Service Book*.

S.C.M. Press Ltd. for the prayer 'We thank you that Jesus was born' (p. 38), The Giving of the Ring(s) (p. 73), the prayer 'We praise and adore you...' (adapted) (p. 110), all from *Contemporary Prayers for Public Worship*.

Central Board of Finance of the General Synod of the Church of England for the prayer 'Blessed be God the Father' (adapted) (p. 74).

Huub Oosterhuis for Thanksgiving III (p. 34).

Oxford and Cambridge University Press for selected passages from *The New English Bible*, second edition © 1970.

The American Bible Society for selected passages from *The Good News Bible*, Old Testament Copyright © 1976, New Testament Copyright © 1966, 1971, 1976.

National Council of the Churches of Christ for selected passages from *The Revised Standard Version of the Bible* © 1946, 1952, 1971, 1973.

Extracts from the Authorised Version of the Bible, which is Crown Copyright, are used with permission.